Legends of
RUGBY

PAUL**MORGAN** and ALEX**MEAD**

Legends of
RUGBY

This revised edition first published in the UK in 2007

© Green Umbrella Publishing 2007

All rights reserved. No part of this work may be reproduced or utilised in any form or by any means, electronic or mechanical, including photocopying, recording by any information storage, and retrieval system, without prior written permission of the Publisher.

Printed and bound in China

ISBN: 978-1-905828-31-9

The views in this book are those of the authors but they are general views only and readers are urged to consult the relevant and qualified specialist for individual advice in particular situations.

Green Umbrella Publishing hereby exclude all liability to the extent permitted by law of any errors or omissions in this book and for any loss, damage or expense (whether direct or indirect) suffered by a third party relying on any information contained in this book.

All our best endeavours have been made to secure copyright clearance for every photograph used but in the event of any copyright owner being overlooked please address correspondence to Green Umbrella Publishing, The Old Bakehouse, 21 The Street, Lydiard Millicent, Swindon SN5 3LU

CONTENTS

Legends of RUGBY

ROB **ANDREW** — 6–9	MIKE **GIBSON** — 62–65	GEORGE **NEPIA** — 112–113
PHIL **BENNETT** — 10–13	GEORGE **GREGAN** — 66–67	BRIAN **O'DRISCOLL** — 114–115
SERGE **BLANCO** — 14–17	GAVIN **HASTINGS** — 68–71	FABIEN **PELOUS** — 116–117
ZINZAN **BROOKE** — 18–19	ANDY **IRVINE** — 72–75	FRANCOIS **PIENAAR** — 118–121
DAVID **CAMPESE** — 20–23	NEIL **JENKINS** — 76–79	HUGO **PORTA** — 122–123
WILL **CARLING** — 24–27	BARRY **JOHN** — 80–81	FRIK **DU PREEZ** — 124–125
DANIE **CRAVEN** — 28–29	MARTIN **JOHNSON** — 82–85	JEAN-PIERRE **RIVES** — 126–127
GERALD **DAVIES** — 30–31	MICHAEL **JONES** — 86–87	PHILIPPE **SELLA** — 128–131
JONATHAN **DAVIES** — 32–35	NICK **FARR-JONES** — 88–91	WAISALE **SEREVI** — 132–135
LAWRENCE **DALLAGLIO** — 36–39	DAVID **KIRK** — 92–93	FERGUS **SLATTERY** — 136–139
DIEGO **DOMINGUEZ** — 40–41	JACKIE **KYLE** — 94–95	GREGOR **TOWNSEND** — 140–141
JOHN **EALES** — 42–43	JASON **LEONARD** — 96–99	RORY **UNDERWOOD** — 142–145
GARETH **EDWARDS** — 44–47	BRIAN **LOCHORE** — 100–101	JONNY **WILKINSON** — 146–149
IEUAN **EVANS** — 48–51	JONAH **LOMU** — 102–105	CHESTER **WILLIAMS** — 150–151
SEAN **FITZPATRICK** — 52–55	WILLIE JOHN **MCBRIDE** — 106–107	JPR **WILLIAMS** — 152–155
GRANT **FOX** — 56–59	COLIN **MEADS** — 108–109	KEITH **WOOD** — 156–157
DAVE **GALLAHER** — 60–61	CLIFF **MORGAN** — 110–111	

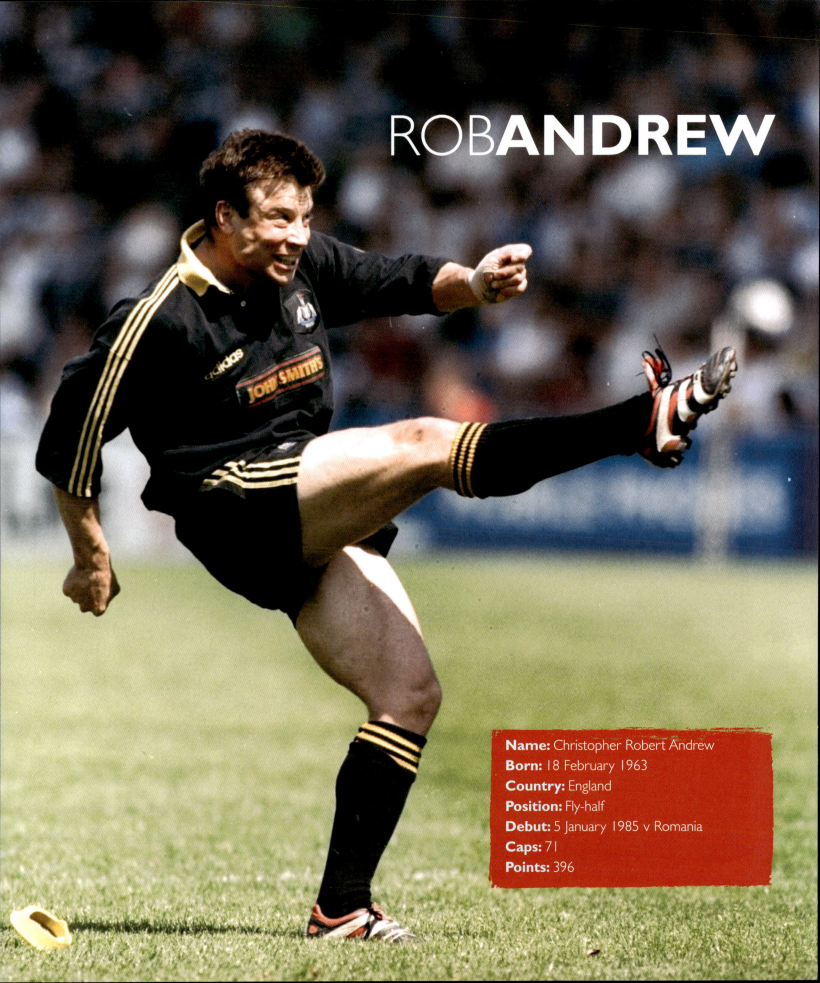

ROB ANDREW

When England's 1995 World Cup quarter-final against Australia moved into stoppage-time, they called on one player to dig them out of the hole – fly-half Rob Andrew. The Wasps man didn't let his side down and when Dewi Morris passed to his team-mate, Andrew bisected the posts from 40 metres out with one of the sweetest drop-goal strikes you could hope to see. It sent England through 25-22 and confirmed Andrew's place in the pantheon of England rugby legends. "I have never seen a drop-goal like that," said England captain Will Carling. "Rob's kicking has been just incredible.

It gives us all so much confidence. We were all trying desperately to avoid extra-time but when he hit it, I didn't have much hope.

Instead, it kept going up and up and up. We knew this would be a huge game and it took a huge drop-goal to win it." Andrew, however, was far more than a drop-goal expert and he built his reputation as one of the best kicking fly-halves in the sport, winning 71 caps for England and five for the Lions. A few months before he sent England through to the semi-finals of the World Cup, he had delivered their third Grand Slam in five years. Needing a last-round win against Scotland, Andrew landed a drop-goal and seven penalties to see England home 24-12, equalling the record for an individual in a Five Nations game.

A pupil of Barnard Castle, he made his senior club debut with Middlesbrough while still at school and was one of the last players in a long line to play for Cambridge University and then go on to represent England.

He captained the Light Blues to victory in the 1985 Varsity Match and was awarded Blues in both rugby and cricket. Indeed, he nearly pursued a professional cricket career, once scoring a century against Nottinghamshire at Trent Bridge. From university, he established his name at Wasps, helping the club become English Champions in 1990. His international career, which saw him become the most-capped fly-half in the world, didn't develop without controversy. For most of his career he competed head-to-head with Bath's Stuart Barnes. The two men were poles apart, Barnes being the master of the running, attacking game and Andrew relying more on his precision kicking, and England's 10-man style, to prosper.

Whatever the merits of Barnes's game, nobody can deny that Andrew's more pragmatic style paid handsome dividends on the Test stage. In the decade before his emergence, England struggled in so many ways and Andrew was the perfect fly-half for the Geoff Cooke-Carling era. With an unrivalled pack of forwards, Andrew was the hand on the tiller and when the forwards forced penalties from their opposition, there was Andrew to slot them over.

During his time England won Grand Slams in 1991, 1992 and 1995, as well as reaching the 1991 World Cup final. He ended his career as the leading point-scorer in England's history, with 396, a record later eclipsed by his protégé Jonny Wilkinson. Andrew had made an instant impact on Test rugby. He made a record-breaking debut in 1984 against Romania, scoring 18 points in a 22-15 victory. That day he scored the first of his 21 Test drop-goals (after just 50 seconds), a record that still stands,

BELOW
Andrew is tracked by Sean Fitzpatrick (2) and Michael Jones during the second Test between The Lions and New Zealand in 1993.

Legends of **RUGBY**

ROB ANDREW

and by the end of the 2006 RBS Six Nations not even Wilkinson had been able to close in on his caps total as a fly-half. Andrew wasn't always England's first-choice goalkicker, either. Bath's Jonathan Webb and Nottingham's Simon Hodgkinson both had stints before Andrew took over on a permanent basis. In 1994, he set a record for most points in a Test match, with 30 against Canada.

Other records followed, including a 'full house' of a try, drop-goal, two conversions and five penalties in a 32-15 win over South Africa in Pretoria. A Lion in 1989 and 1993, Andrew was crucial to the side's series win in Australia, on his first tour. He missed the initial selection but, after an injury to Paul Dean, took his chance by winning the battle for the No 10 jersey with Scotland's Craig Chalmers. After the Lions lost the first Test, it was Andrew's kicking that underpinned their 19-12 win. He was also one of the successes of a losing tour to New Zealand four years later. Andrew, who also had brief sojourns playing for Australian club Gordon and Toulouse, wasn't content with the huge effect he'd had merely as a player.

When the game turned professional in 1995, he became player-coach at Newcastle, a club that had just been bought by the millionaire Sir John Hall. Within three years, Andrew had guided his new club to the Premiership title, and Powergen Cup triumphs were to follow in 2001 and 2004. His move north precipitated his retirement from international rugby, at 32, but he was called back into service one more time, after an injury to Paul Grayson saw Andrew called up for

Legends of **RUGBY**

FAR LEFT
Andrew lines up to kick the ball for England during the Five Nations match against Scotland played at Twickenham, 1989.

LEFT
Rob Andrew powers forward for England during a match against Fiji, 1991.

BELOW
Andrew with the Five Nations trophy, in 1995, after England had completed their third Grand Slam in five years.

England's visit to Wales in March 1997. He retired as a player completely after dislocating a shoulder in 1999. When he made his decision to quit in 1995, it was clear he was capable of staying in the England jersey for years to come. "I am stunned at Rob's retirement," said England manager Jack Rowell. "It leaves a huge gap in the England firmament.

His performances have got better as he has got older." Even as a club coach, Andrew's influence on the England team didn't dwindle as he was responsible for the development of Wilkinson, who moved to Newcastle from school and grew into an England international under Andrew's tutelage.

A respected rugby analyst for The Daily Mail and BBC radio, in 2005 he completed a decade as director of rugby at Newcastle. The following year he was linked with a move into the England management structure after an awful Six Nations campaign, but he quickly quelled such speculation by declaring his commitment to the Falcons.

Legends of **RUGBY**

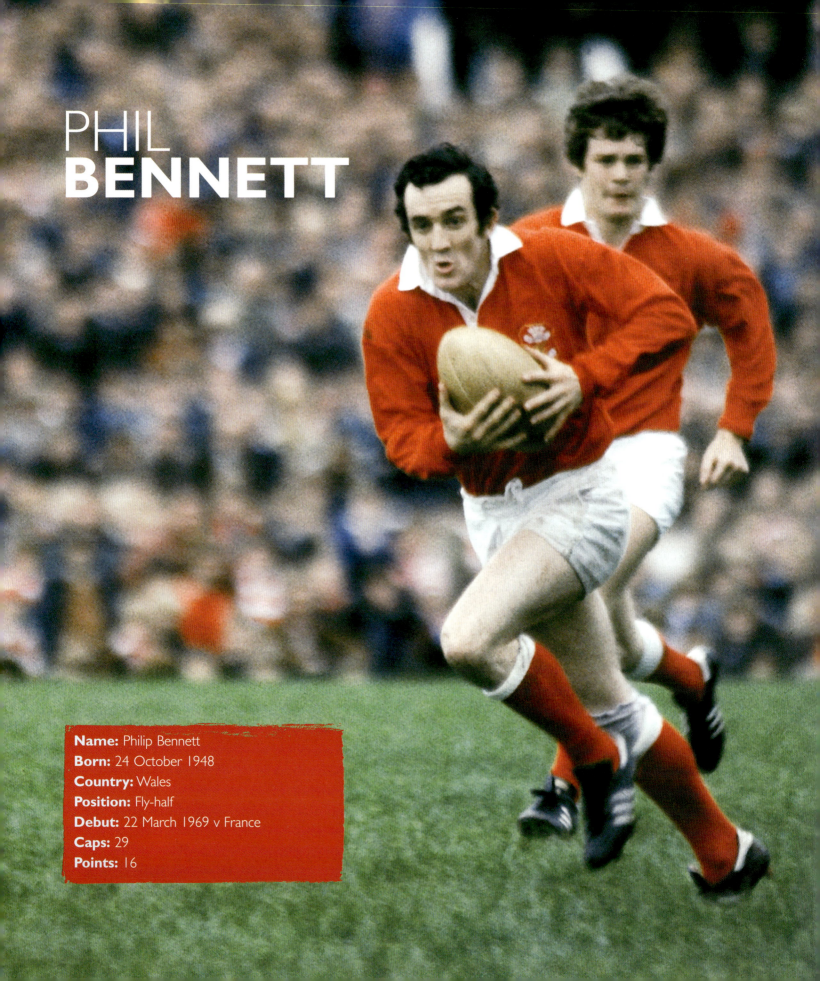

PHIL BENNETT

Name: Philip Bennett
Born: 24 October 1948
Country: Wales
Position: Fly-half
Debut: 22 March 1969 v France
Caps: 29
Points: 16

PHIL BENNETT

Two Lions tours stand head and shoulders above the rest: the vintage of 1971 and 1974, when they won in New Zealand and South Africa respectively. The 1974 Lions won a titanic Test series, 3-0 with the final match drawn, and they achieved that historic triumph against the Springboks with a magician at outside-half, Llanelli's Phil Bennett.

The man with the stunning sidestep and an almost unerring right boot left an indelible mark on rugby union. Against the Boks, he formed a dream partnership with Gareth Edwards at half-back, and he was to score more than 100 points on the tour. His 50-yard try in the second Test in Pretoria, which the Lions won 28-9, will live with all who saw it, Bennett finishing it off with a final sidestep that left full-back Ian McCallum utterly bamboozled. Many regarded this as the game of Bennett's life. And on his return to Britain, rugby league came calling, St Helens offering him £40,000 over a three-year period – a vast sum in those days.

The man known throughout the rugby world as Benny turned them down, just as he had refused an offer from Halifax when Bennett was still playing youth rugby for his village team as a 17-year-old.

Within weeks of his triumphant homecoming from South Africa, Bennett's life turned upside down as he and his wife Pat lost their first child, Stewart, because of a heart defect.

For a time rugby meant nothing to Bennett, but he slowly came to terms with the tragedy, and by 1977 he agreed to tour again with the Lions – this time as captain. He thus became only the second Welshman, after John Dawes, to lead a genuine Lions squad.

That trip to New Zealand proved an exacting one for the tourists as they lost the series 3-1, although Bennett still managed to score 100 points on the tour.

His famous sidestep has become celebrated across the world and in 1973 he was the chief architect of the game's most famous try, scored by the Barbarians against New Zealand at Cardiff Arms Park.

Simply referred to today as 'that try', Bennett started a legendary length-of-the-field move with some mesmerizing sidesteps near his own try-line to turn defence into attack, and several passes later the move was completed when Edwards dived over in the corner.

There was huge pressure on Bennett right from the start of his international career as he was asked to take over the famed Wales No 10 jersey from The King, Barry John.

"That was a tough act to follow but the Llanelli wizard rose to the challenge," remembered Ireland international Phil Matthews in The Sunday Times. "His 50-metre try in the second Test at Pretoria saw him swerve and sidestep through the Springbok defence in a way I could only dream of repeating."

But take over from John he did, with all the panache expected of a Welsh fly-half, winning 29 caps for Wales, eight of them as captain.

Bennett made his Test debut in 1969 during an 8-8 draw with France, becoming the first Welsh replacement to be capped.

With John in the side, some of his early Test rugby was spent at full-back, but after inheriting the No 10 jersey he prospered and by the time Bennett retired from

BELOW
Phil Bennett kicks for touch during a match for the Lions against Wellington, New Zealand 1977.

PHIL BENNETT

international rugby in 1978, he held the Welsh scoring record, with 166 points.

Bennett's glory days weren't restricted to the Lions. He won three Grand Slams and four Triple Crowns with Wales, while he enjoyed 16 wonderful seasons with Llanelli, the Scarlets winning four successive Welsh Cup finals from 1973-76.

He also helped manufacture the most famous victory in Llanelli's history, as they beat the All Blacks 9-3 in 1972.

Delme Thomas, the Llanelli captain that day, remembered a piece of Bennett magic when he recently spoke to the Western Mail. As Bennett received the ball to make a clearance to touch, he found himself staring into the combative eyes of Grant Batty, the quick and uncompromising All Black winger who had come on as a replacement for Bryan Williams.

Bennett, with one of those magical sidesteps, glided past Batty before kicking to touch.

"I'll never forget the look on Batty's face as he clutched at empty air," Thomas said. "It was the moment I knew we had won."

Bill McLaren, the famous rugby commentator, summed up what so many thought about Bennett. "His adhesive hands, his educated boot, his nose for space and those shimmering sidesteps… could light up a game with pure genius," said McLaren.

Bennett ended his international career on an emotional high, captaining the Wales team of 1978 to a Grand Slam. In the final game, the great man scored two tries in a 16-7 victory over France at Cardiff. "The crowd won the game for us that day," he said. "Yes, the boys

FAR LEFT
Bennett in action during the Test Series between New Zealand and the British Lions in July 1977.

LEFT
Bennett, Lions Captain, leads out his team to play Waikato in Hamilton, New Zealand, 1977.

BELOW
Bennett kicks to touch during the British Lions tour match against South Africa, 1974.

played with huge spirit but that emotional singing from the crowd made it. Once they started, there was no way France were ever going to score.

"I'd decided before the game that I would retire. I'd had a couple of good seasons, the crowd were very nice to me and I thought, 'Why spoil it by hanging on?'" Bennett was just 29 when he took his curtain call.

With Bennett and several other Wales stars retiring at that time, it took the Principality 27 years to win another Grand Slam.

Bennett was a man full of humility and he was delighted by his recent induction into the International Rugby Hall of Fame.

"To be inducted alongside the likes of Gareth Edwards, Gerald Davies and Mervyn Davies is such an honour," said Bennett. "It makes me feel very humble when I think back to my days playing for Felinfoel Youth, Llanelli Schoolboys, my beloved Scarlets and Wales."

Bennett moved into broadcasting after his playing days were over and he now commentates on the game for television.

Legends of **RUGBY**

SERGE BLANCO

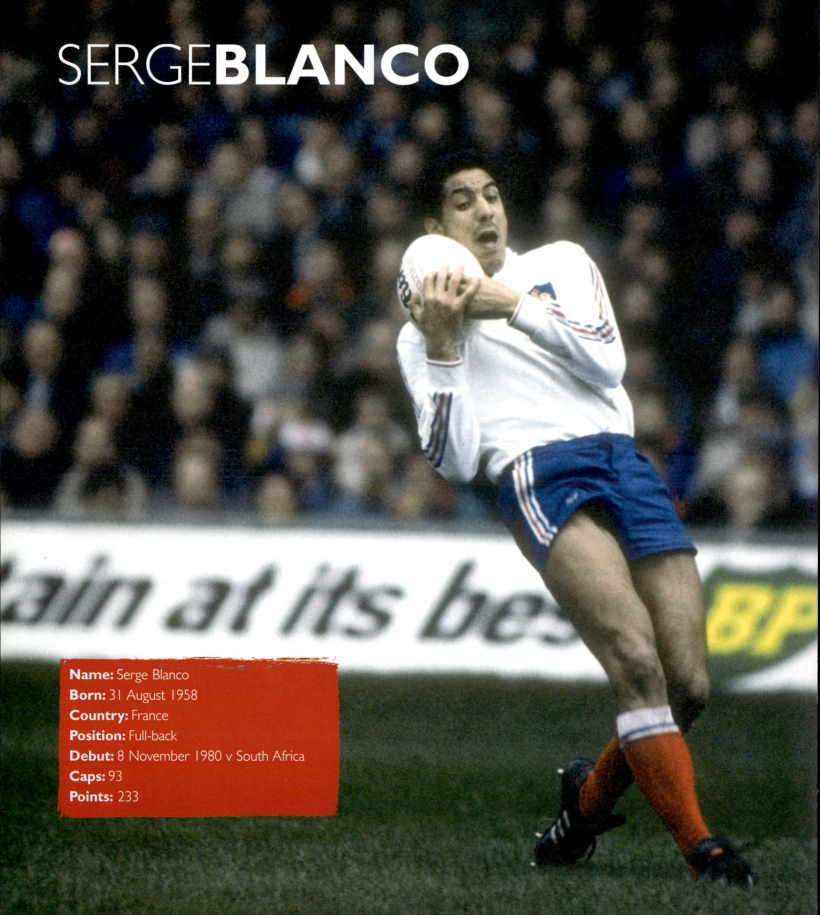

Name: Serge Blanco
Born: 31 August 1958
Country: France
Position: Full-back
Debut: 8 November 1980 v South Africa
Caps: 93
Points: 233

SERGE BLANCO

In every era comes a player who sums up the soul of a rugby team. In the 1980s that role belonged to Serge Blanco, the mercurial French international who defined everything good about his side in that decade. Born in 1958 in Venezuela, Blanco had no peer in the No 15 jersey at that time and only a handful in the history of rugby.

He won a staggering 93 caps for France, after his family moved to the country when he was a child. Blanco's versatility was evident by the fact that he won 12 of those caps on the wing, while he is regarded as the iconic full-back, winning a place in Rugby World's Team of the Century. He had pace to spare and at 6ft 1in and approaching 14st he had the power to make him one of the most elusive full-backs to play the game. His ability to change speed also made him a nightmare for opponents.

Luckily for Blanco, the World Cup kicked off while he was in his pomp and although New Zealand won the first tournament in 1987, for many the fondest memory is Blanco's try in the semi-final against Australia, when he battled injury to send his side through.

In front of just 18,000 spectators at Sydney's Concord Oval and with the game locked at 24-24, Blanco struck. Receiving the ball 30 metres out, he flew towards the corner on an angled run, scoring with a full-length dive to beat Tommy Lawton. Didier Camberabero's touchline conversion gave France a 30-24 victory.

John Reason, writing in The Daily Telegraph, said: "I never thought I would see a game to rival the one played between the Barbarians and the All Blacks in Cardiff in 1973, but this one did.

"The French came back from 9-0, 15-12 and 24-21 down and then at the death a surging move involving Champ, Lagisquet, Berbizier, Mesnel, Charvet, Berbezier again and Lagisquet again saw Rodriguez in support and Blanco forgetting his injured hamstring and going for his life and a try in the corner to put France in the final."

That try was typical of Blanco – who captained France 17 times – and the French of that era. Flair emanated from all parts of the team and the plaudits were quick to follow. France not only reached that first World Cup final but won Grand Slams in 1981 and 1987, as well as taking at least a share of the Five Nations Championship a further four times in the Eighties.

Blanco made his Test debut against South Africa in Cape Town in 1980 and although the French lost 37-15, it was the start of an 11-year career that brought him a France record of 38 tries, a tally that remained unbeaten by any full-back as the 2006 Six Nations drew to a close.

Blanco's elegant running style, creativity and inventive spirit epitomised the flamboyance for which French rugby is admired. He was an 'old school' player, smoking 60 cigarettes a day throughout his career (he gave up a year after retiring from the game), and still turning in performances that shook the rugby world.

David Campese is a player in the same mould as Blanco and the great Aussie often lamented the change of attitude that arrived with professionalism. "The emphasis is on winning, not entertaining," Campese said. "The creative aspect has gone and so have the

BELOW
Serge Blanco kicks for goal as Rob Andrew of England tries to block during a match at Twickenham in 1985.

Legends of **RUGBY**

SERGE BLANCO

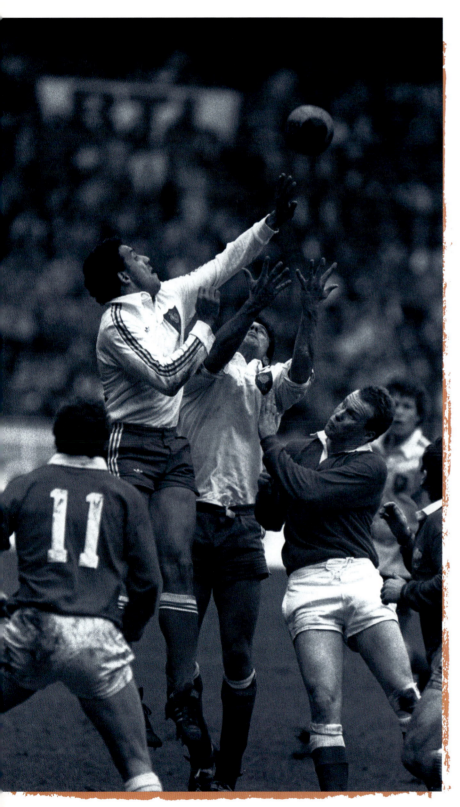

characters, people like Serge Blanco, who always seemed to play with a smile on his face. Now it's a job. They're all told what to say and what not to say."

No one could have told a free spirit like Blanco what to do. Attacking from his own line and creating a try out of nothing were commonplace to him, no matter how big the occasion. In 1991, England and France met at Twickenham in a Grand Slam decider. Just 12 minutes into the game, Blanco lit the blue touchpaper for one of the greatest tries ever seen when he fielded a missed penalty attempt and launched a 100-yard counter-attack, which ended with Philippe Saint-Andre scoring under the posts.

His philosophy on the game is simple. "There are too many outside interests ruling the game and the financial rewards for the television companies and federations apply great pressure on teams to win," Blanco said. "The only way to make rugby a spectacle again is to make sure players are encouraged to express themselves."

Rugby was cruel to Blanco at the end, his final Test bringing defeat as France lost to England in the 1991 World Cup quarter-final in Paris.

But at least he bowed out in England in style, making a dazzling, try-scoring appearance in December 1991 as the Barbarians beat Leicester 29-21 in the annual Christmas holiday fixture.

Steve Bale, writing in The Independent, summed up his impact: "People talk about Blanco's supposed shortage of speed but his capacity for opening up defences with power and acceleration, mesmerising changes of pace and direction, and the most delicate

FAR LEFT
Honours flowed in Blanco's magnificent career.

LEFT
Blanco on the charge for France during the 1991 Five Nations Championship match between Wales.

BELOW
Blanco was a hugely athletic full-back.

passing subtlety seemed completely unimpaired yesterday. As he will not play in England again, it was a privilege to watch the last farewell. Keeping such a man under control is asking the impossible."

Blanco's final club game ended in similar fashion, his beloved Biarritz losing the 1992 national championship final to Toulon.

But there was no way Blanco was going to leave the sport forever. He became president of Biarritz Olympique, seeing them become French champions in 2002.

He was also made president of France's national professional league, the Ligue Nationale de Rugby, ensuring his status as one of the most powerful men in the game.

Life outside rugby has seen him open the Serge Blanco Hotel and Thalassotherapy Centre in Hendaye in 1991 (other hotels have followed), and in 1992 The Serge Blanco range, with its striking 15 logo, was launched, leading to the opening of 50 shops.

Legends of **RUGBY**

ZINZAN BROOKE

With an All Blacks points tally that includes 17 tries and three drop-goals, it's obvious that Zinzan Brooke was at the front of the line when God was dishing out rugby skills.

As for what made him so great, well, he had the classic New Zealand upbringing. His first love wasn't rugby but sheep-shearing and by the time he was a teenager he was able to shear hundreds of them a day – a talent that no doubt helped build up the strength he later displayed on the world's rugby fields. "Those days I wanted to be a Golden Shears champion," he once said. "The All Blacks weren't a serious consideration. I loved the oily smell and feel of the wool and the battle with the rams and the cranky ewes."

Talented as he was at sheep-shearing, there was always a rugby ball around the farm to play with and, without it being thrust upon him, he took to the game in a big way. He made his senior debut for Warkworth at the tender age of 15 – and ran in three tries. Brooke was clearly something a bit special – a fact that's been acknowledged by many over the years. Not least John Hart, the man in charge of the All Blacks when Brooke made his final Test appearance in 1997. "There is no other player that has the range of skills, including drop-kicking, in the loose forwards that this fellow has," said Hart. "He has brought abilities to loose-forward play that no other player has brought. He has done things that no player can do. He is immensely competitive but he also has immense flair.

"He's one of the hardest men you could get, and you don't often get the mixture of absolute hardness and flair. The other unique issue is his tactical appreciation. He has an unbelievable grasp of the game." But before he could earn such lavish praise from the coach of the world's most famous rugby side, Brooke had a lot of work to do.

After his club debut, he turned out for the North Island Under-16s at prop and later made his first appearance – also at prop – in the black shirt of New Zealand with the under-17 national side against Australia.

While studying to be a plumber in Auckland, Brooke opted for the Marist club and it was from here that he would find his way onto the representative scene. It was with the Auckland sevens side that he made a name for himself, the abridged game allowing him to show off his full repertoire. His high point in sevens proved to be the Hong Kong tournament where he joined the likes of Buck Shelford, Frano Botica and David Kirk in a Kiwi side that would beat the French Barbarians in the final to take the title.

Name: Zinzan Valentine Brooke
Born: 14 February 1965
Country: New Zealand
Position: No 8
Debut: 1 June 1987 v Argentina
Caps: 58
Points: 89

Legends of **RUGBY**

ZINZAN BROOKE

By this time Brooke had been moved from the tight to the loose forwards by his Marist coach and he was also allowed to kick goals for his club – a move which would pay dividends for the All Blacks and Auckland years later.

A full New Zealand cap came his way in 1987 – in the inaugural World Cup – against Argentina. Despite scoring a try and putting in a decent performance, the young Brooke didn't impress everyone. "He possesses special skills but he will never make it as an openside flanker," said Graham Mourie in a newspaper column.

Not making it at openside flanker, however, didn't prove much of a stumbling block for Brooke. The presence of the legendary Shelford, however, did and as a result Brooke made few starts until 1990. When he was chosen over Shelford, it caused public outrage of a scale rarely seen even in New Zealand rugby. "It was a little unfortunate that I should have eventually been chosen to replace Buck," said Brooke. "At the time I was considering an offer to play rugby league in Australia, but people in the know told me that if I held on I could expect the No 8 shirt to come my way. I can't say I liked the fact that I knew Buck's fate before he did. And the public weren't too happy, either. People wrote letters to newspapers, called radio stations to complain. At virtually every ground I went to, people would be holding up 'Bring Back Buck' banners. Even after Buck had retired."

The public wasn't to know of the influence that Shelford's successor would have on the game. Even when being benched by the All Blacks, he was still crossing the whitewash with the regularity of a flying winger.

When he managed to convert his try-scoring skills to the international arena, he began to win over the public. Unfortunately, he would also suffer – alongside his team-mates – the pain of three defeats to the Wallabies, the last of which came in the 1991 World Cup semi-final in Dublin.

In the post-World Cup shake-up, Brooke looked to be on his way out, but new coach Laurie Mains was persuaded to change his mind by Sean Fitzpatrick, who said of him: "He's a great player who will play whatever game you ask of him. The reason he's been so loose is because he's had no direction in playing for Auckland."

The ringing endorsement did the trick and Brooke was handed his All Black lifeline.

Injuries continued to play their part in his career, but he rallied one last time at the 1995 World Cup, landing a sensational drop-goal against England in the semi-final. However, the All Blacks suffered food poisoning before the final and lost to South Africa in extra-time.

Brooke returned the following year and this time made sure of things with his try and drop-goal in Pretoria helping to defeat the world champions during an historic series win.

A year later he retired from the international scene, making his final appearance against England before making the country his home and signing for Premiership outfit Harlequins.

LEFT
All Black Zinzan Brooke dives in for a try during the Bledisloe Cup played between New Zealand and the Wallabies.

BELOW
Brooke pushes off Wallaby Andrew Blades in the tri-nations match, 1997.

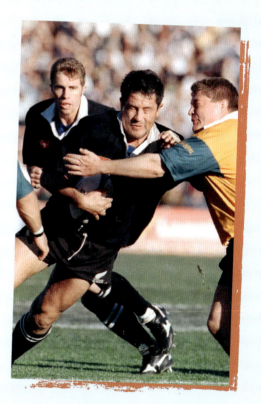

Legends of **RUGBY**

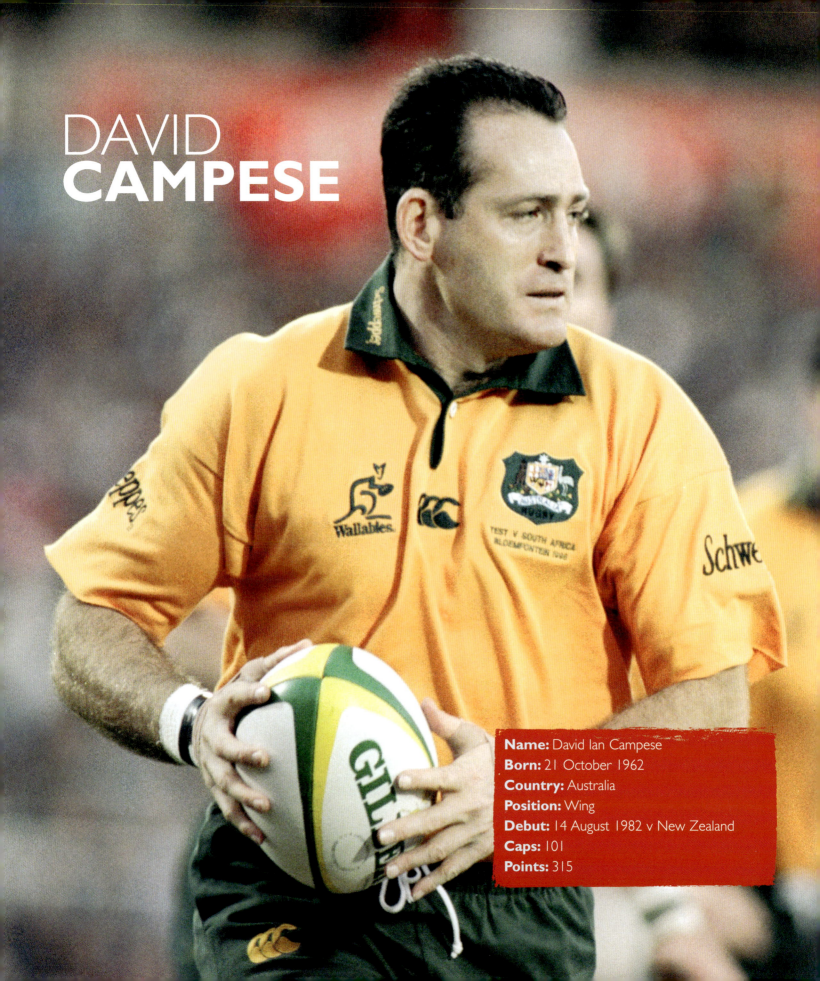

DAVID CAMPESE

Name: David Ian Campese
Born: 21 October 1962
Country: Australia
Position: Wing
Debut: 14 August 1982 v New Zealand
Caps: 101
Points: 315

DAVID CAMPESE

David Campese played his last Test for the Wallabies in December 1996, and so prolific was he that his world record of 64 tries was still unsurpassed, and in fact not even threatened by anyone in the top 10 nations, a decade later. The winger started life on the international stage in 1982 – long before the Super 14 – at his club Randwick. And he went on to win a sensational 101 caps for Australia, lifting the 1991 World Cup along the way.

But it wasn't just his try-scoring (and the occasional drop-goal) that ensured Campese, who is of Italian descent, stood out from the crowd. It was his style and his approach to the game, from his trademark goose-step to the way he would attack from places where others wouldn't dare – even from behind his own posts.

His finest hour came in that 1991 World Cup in Europe. He failed to score in the final as Australia beat England 12-6 at Twickenham, but he had already illuminated the tournament with a brilliant display in the semi-final against New Zealand at Lansdowne Road.

"Campese brought the sparkle back to rugby in the twinkling of a few star-studded strides," wrote John Mason of The Daily Telegraph, commenting on that 16-6 semi-final victory. "In routing the peddlers of caution, the purveyors of the unimaginative and second-rate, the extraordinary Campese also brought down New Zealand, the world champions."

His try was sumptuous, the right-wing popping up on the left to take a pass from Nick Farr-Jones, break the All Blacks line and arrow to the corner.

But the second was even better. Campo (as he is known throughout the world of rugby) made it with a nonchalant flip pass over his shoulder, centre Tim Horan accepting the gift to scurry over and leave the Kiwis too big a mountain to climb. It was a sublime moment from a rugby genius.

Although he didn't score in the final, Campese had a significant hand in the victory. His comments in the run-up to the game were credited with forcing England to change their style. Will Carling's team had rumbled through to the final with a forward-dominated game plan, but Campese teased them in the days prior to the big match, helping to create the pressure that prompted a sudden change in England's philosophy. England's attempts to use their backs more in the final backfired and, despite a clear supremacy up front, the men in white were to finish as losers.

Campese's own philosophy throughout his career was simple. "I don't know what I'm going to do next, so how can anyone else?" he once said, high-lighting in a nutshell the problems opponents had trying to curb his wondrous talents.

He ended the 1991 World Cup with six of Australia's 17 tries and was voted Player of the Tournament. Campese grew up outside Canberra before moving to Sydney, making his international debut aged 19 against New Zealand at Christchurch in 1982. He kicked off with a try, too, as Australia lost 23-16.

He scored again against the All Blacks two weeks later, in an historic 19-16 win for the Wallabies in Wellington, ensuring he was well and truly on the rugby world map.

BELOW
Campese gives out a few final instructions during the Australia versus Wales game at Cardiff Arms Park in 1996.

Legends of **RUGBY**

DAVID CAMPESE

That chance came after Campese showed outstanding form in the ACT and Australia Under-21s sides, and his break came when a number of Wallabies withdrew from that 1982 trip to New Zealand. He never looked back.

In the UK he left an indelible mark long before that World Cup as he was part of a new breed of Australia player: one of a group that helped win a Grand Slam (tour victories over England, Scotland, Ireland and Wales) for the Wallabies in 1984.

Campese was aided and abetted by a group of world-class Wallabies on that 1984 tour, including Michael Lynagh, Mark Ella and Nick Farr-Jones. Those four victories, which started with a 19-3 win at Twickenham against England, ensured the Wallabies' place in the new world order.

His duals with New Zealand were the stuff of legend, and in 1986 he helped Australia to their first Bledisloe Cup triumph in New Zealand for 37 years.

But it wasn't all glory for Campo because, like many geniuses, he had his flaws. His most famous blunder cost Australia the 1989 series against the Lions. In the third Test, he tried to initiate a counter-attack from behind his own try-line, was struck by a moment of indecision and threw a risky pass to full-back Greg Martin. The ball went to ground and Ieuan Evans pounced to win the Test – and the series – for the Lions.

Campese was pilloried by some for the error, but most rugby fans saw sense, realising that one or two flaws in his make-up was a small price to pay for such outrageous ability. Lions and England centre Jeremy Guscott said: "Campese tries things, and that is part of his genius. Remove the risk and he would be half the player."

Legends of **RUGBY**

FAR LEFT
The world's most prolific try-scorer, Campese powers through against Italy.

LEFT
David Campese leaves the field after his final match, during the Australian tour against the Barbarians at Twickenham, 1996.

BELOW
Campese was a huge fan of Sevens, here in action against Scotland in 1993.

Campese became the first Australian to play 100 Tests when the Wallabies took on Italy in 1996 and a few weeks later he played his final Test, at Cardiff Arms Park against Wales. He failed to score but the Wallabies ensured a winning send-off for Campo, with a 28-19 victory.

A great advocate of sevens, Campese helped Australia to a Hong Kong Sevens title in 1983 and went on to coach the national sevens team to the bronze medal in the 1998 Commonwealth Games in Malaysia.

After holding a number of other coaching roles, in 2006 he was appointed as a consultant for South Africa's Sharks in the Super 14.

In January 2002, he was awarded the Order of Australia Medal for his services to rugby, and he still owns a sports shop, near Sydney Harbour.

Legends of **RUGBY**

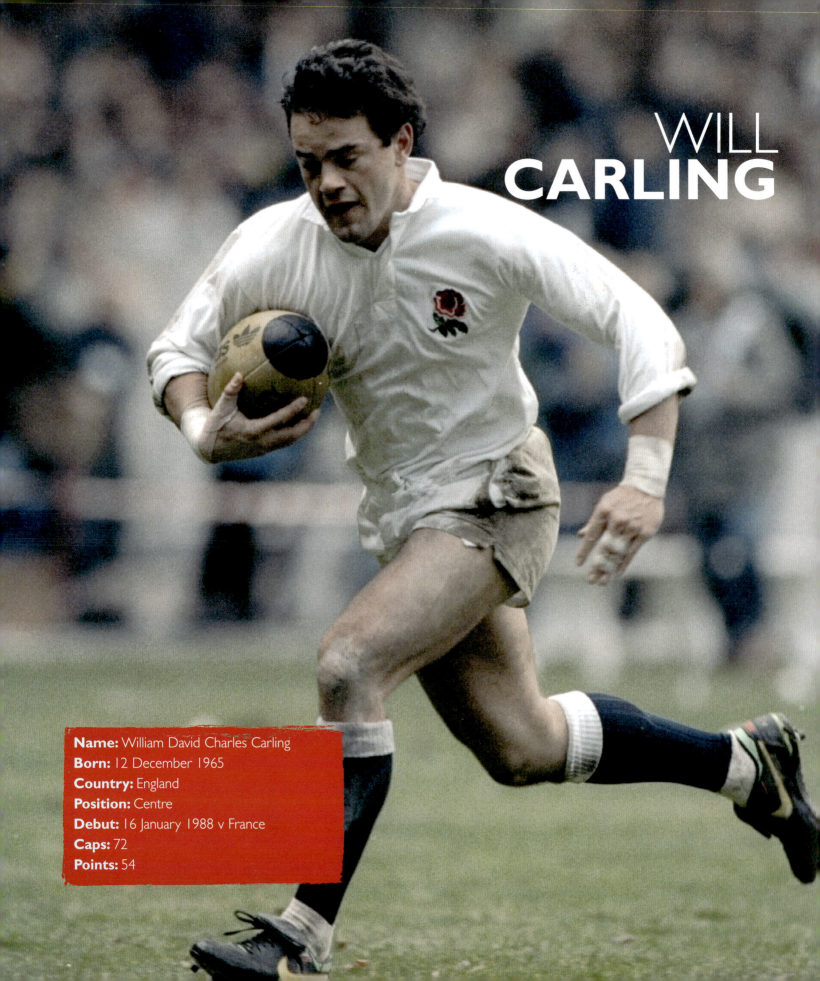

WILL CARLING

Name: William David Charles Carling
Born: 12 December 1965
Country: England
Position: Centre
Debut: 16 January 1988 v France
Caps: 72
Points: 54

WILL CARLING

It says something of the British press that Will Carling is as famous for his off-the-field activities as he is for his many achievements on the green fields of English rugby. Educated at Sedbergh and Durham University, Carling made his name on the club scene with Harlequins, with whom he won the John Player Cup in 1988 and the Pilkington Cup three years later.

A powerful runner and superb in defence, Carling was the perfect foil in England's midfield for the graceful, silky skills of Jeremy Guscott, and the pair enjoyed a partnership that took to the field on 44 occasions from 1989 to 1996.

It was a different talent that made Carling stand out from the crowd, though – an ability to lead. He made his England debut against France in January 1988 and by the end of the year was leading his country out at Twickenham to face Australia – having been handed the captain's armband by coach Geoff Cooke.

While many doubted the wisdom of putting such pressure on the shoulders of a 22-year-old, Cooke's gamble paid off as England saw off the Wallabies 28-19. It was a game that marked a sea change in England's fortunes with the national side having endured a monumental slump since the early 1980s.

Carling helped England finish joint second in the 1989 Five Nations, and the following year a Grand Slam loomed as he led the country to wins over Wales, Ireland and France – leaving just Scotland to come. But it wasn't to be, as the Scots decided the Grand Slam was to be theirs that year and beat the auld enemy 13-7. It was a win that hurts Carling still. "I can barely remember the dinner [after the game] because I was in such a state of shock that I couldn't even drink myself into oblivion; it was weird. Looking across the room at the Scots' celebrations, I thought, 'If I never, ever lose to these bastards again, I'll be happy' – and I never did. But I also never got over it."

But from adversity you often find triumph and this was the case for Carling's England. Despite defeat, England were on the up, their success based on a formidable pack and the pinpoint accuracy of Rob Andrew's boot. When the ball did go down the back-line, the likes of Guscott, Carling and Rory Underwood were on hand to make the breaks and apply the finishing touches.

Timing is everything, though, and England timed their first Grand Slam for over a decade to perfection as 1991 was also World Cup year. Still hurting from their Murrayfield failure, England set upon the 1991 Five Nations with renewed vigour. Wales, a side they hadn't beaten in Cardiff since 1963, were first up and Carling showed his brand of leadership when the England side walked the distance from the hotel to the national stadium. An unusual approach maybe, but it worked a treat as the Welsh were dispatched 25-6 and England were on their way. Scotland fell next, then Ireland and finally France – 21-19 at Twickenham. It was England's first Grand Slam since 1980.

A World Cup on home soil followed later that year and Carling again proved to have what it takes to keep England ticking over as they marched to the final at HQ against Australia. This time, though, England and Carling got it wrong. Seemingly in response to Australia's jibes over their style of play, England changed

BELOW
A portrait of England Rugby Union captain Will Carling during a London photoshoot in 1989.

Legends of **RUGBY**

WILL CARLING

tactics and attempted expansive rugby – a move that cost them the best chance of a world crown.

England did manage to make partial amends with a second Grand Slam in 1992, and with Carling's own game continuing to flourish, he was picked for the Lions tour to New Zealand in 1993. While starting the first Test, he then lost his place to the Welsh centre Scott Gibbs.

Unable to get his its hands on the Five Nations title for the next two seasons, England repeated the Grand Slam trick in 1995, once again the year of the World Cup. Perfect timing.

This time, though, Carling was making headlines for the wrong (or right, depending on your view) reasons as he was caught criticising the powers-that-be in English rugby with the immortal line: "If the game is run properly as a professional game, you do not need 57 old farts running rugby."

While initially he was sacked as captain, with no player willing to take the job on and a World Cup in the offing, he was swiftly reinstated.

At the quarter-final stage, England defeated Champions Australia and Will Carling's men were being touted as possible World Cup Champions. They hadn't counted on Jonah Lomu. The teenage wing – with a bit of help from his fellow New Zealanders – put England to the sword in the semi-final. Carling scored two tries but it was of little consequence as his side were humbled 45-29.

Even without a World Cup, Carling's time as captain – which came to an end the following year after a record 59 appearances as skipper – saw England rise from the ashes to become a true force in world rugby. Not only had they beaten the best of Europe, but they had triumphed over the southern hemisphere superpowers

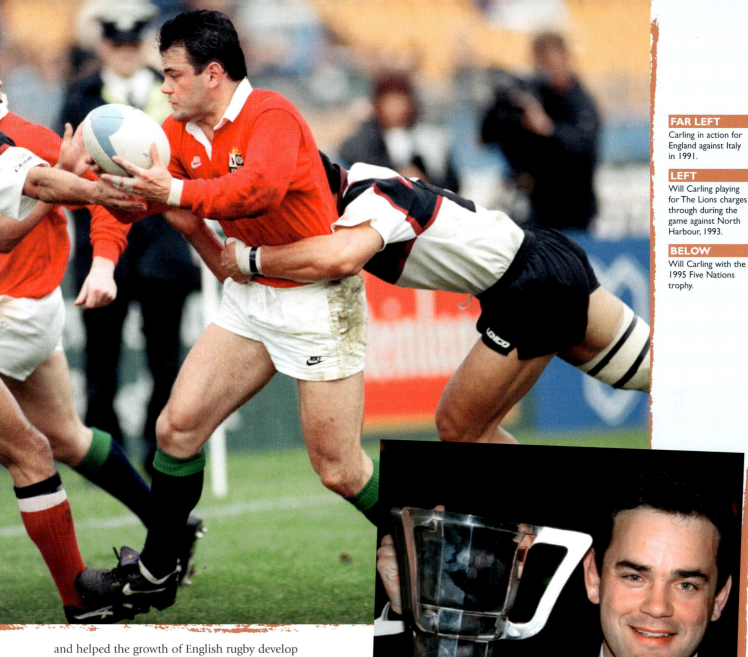

FAR LEFT
Carling in action for England against Italy in 1991.

LEFT
Will Carling playing for The Lions charges through during the game against North Harbour, 1993.

BELOW
Will Carling with the 1995 Five Nations trophy.

and helped the growth of English rugby develop some way into what it is today. Even when he was on the front pages rather than the back, he was still raising the profile of the game. Carling hung up his international boots in 1997, and then his club ones soon after following a bust-up with coach Andy Keast at Harlequins.

He returned a year later when Zinzan Brooke was at the helm of the Stoop, but his comeback was short-lived.

Nonetheless, after three Grand Slams, one World Cup final, four Five Nations titles and five Triple Crowns, Will Carling had certainly done his bit for English rugby.

Legends of **RUGBY**

DANIE CRAVEN

With museums, awards and stadiums named after him, the influence of Daniel (Danie) Hartman Craven on South African rugby was evidently immense. It's rare to find an individual who excelled not only as a player but also as a coach and then a rugby administrator. And from his first cap in 1931 up until his death in 1993, Craven remained one of the pivotal figures at the forefront of South African rugby during its most turbulent times.

Although his playing career spanned just 16 caps – it was curtailed by the onset of World War Two – Craven managed to fit plenty into them.

He made his debut against Wales in 1931 at scrum-half as part of Bennie Osler's team that toured the British Isles. Having overcome Wales 8-3 in Swansea, the side beat Ireland by the same scoreline and then Scotland 6-3, with Craven grabbing his first international try.

It was a taste of things to come for Craven, as winning was something he was to prove adept at both as a player and a coach.

His rugby life was no doubt enhanced by the fact he studied at the famous Stellenbosch University – where the stadium and museum are named after him – and it was during his time there that he earned his first caps.

After the successful tour of the British Isles, Craven went on to play in seven Tests against the Wallabies – winning five of them, including two in Australia on the 1937 tour. It was on that same tour that Craven first captained the Springboks – against the All Blacks in Wellington – and although he was on the wrong side of a 13-7 scoreline, the tide soon turned. With Craven directing operations, the Springboks fought back to beat New Zealand 13-6 and 17-6 to secure an impressive 2-1 Test-series victory.

To add a further element of history-making, Craven appeared at fly-half and No 8 as well as in his usual role of scrum-half – a feat that, together with an earlier appearance in the centre, meant he represented South Africa in an unprecedented four positions in Test rugby. To add to his astonishing versatility, he also had a bash at full-back for a touring match against Queensland.

Craven certainly made the most of his international appearances. As if beating Australia and New Zealand on their own turf wasn't enough, which itself followed an unbeaten three-Test tour of Britain and Ireland, he also managed to fit in the visit of the British & Irish Lions in 1938.

Having assumed the captaincy, Craven led his side to a 2-1 Test-series victory, winning the first two matches 26-12 and 19-3 before succumbing in the third Test – a dead rubber – by 21-16.

The Second World War was then to put a stop to his playing career, but Craven had already achieved a fantastic amount and was widely regarded as the finest scrum-half of his generation. His achievements on the

Name: Daniel Hartman Craven
Born: 11 October 1910
Country: South Africa
Position: Scrum-half
Debut: 5 December 1931 v Wales
Caps: 16
Points: 6

DANIE CRAVEN

LEFT
Craven was president of the South African union for an incredible 37 years.

BELOW
Craven was a leader, known across South Africa as Mr Rugby.

playing field were many, but his off-field involvement would outweigh all of them.

Coaching at his beloved Stellenbosch University from 1947 to 1991, Craven also put his rugby nous to good use for the national side, working as a selector and coach from 1949 until 1956. During his time of influence, the Springboks whitewashed the All Blacks 4-0 and won ten matches in a row. On the 1951-52 tour of Britain, Craven's side not only completed a Grand Slam but also won fans far and wide for their powerful brand of rugby. At Murrayfield the Boks triumphed 44-0 against Scotland – an incredible margin in those times of the three-point try. His influence from the touchline was so great that he's still talked about as one of the finest rugby coaches in Springbok history.

Even after all of this, Craven's devotion and passion for rugby remained as strong as ever and, to satisfy his appetite for the game, he became president of the SA Rugby Board in 1956 and from 1957 represented South Africa on the International Rugby Board – becoming chairman when it was his nation's turn.

His tenure as president was to last 37 years until the day he died and it was a period in which South Africa suffered its most controversial and difficult times as apartheid caused the rest of the world to look upon the country with disdain and eventually boycott them.

Even before their exile, it was a struggle to find games and it was the work of Craven that ensured they did play, fixtures in the Eighties against South America, New Zealand Cavaliers and a World XV giving South Africa's top players a taste of top-class rugby.

The influence of rugby in South African politics was so great that the sometimes-controversial Craven once said: "We can change South Africa on the rugby field." In meeting with the exiled African National Congress, he attempted to do just that.

His lifetime's work came to a fitting conclusion with the unity of the South African Football Union in 1992, a year before he died.

On top of all of his rugby work, Craven managed to gain three doctorates (four if you include the honorary one) in social anthropology, psychology and physical education, he worked as a teacher, soldier and professor, and he found time to pen several books on different aspects of the game, from coaching to history. He was also awarded honorary citizenship of Lindley, his birthplace in the Orange Free State, and Stellenbosch.

Even outside of South Africa, Craven had many admirers, not least Argentina – a side with whom the Springboks now contest the Danie Craven Trophy. At the inaugural contest for the trophy in 2004, the chief executive of Argentina Rugby, Christian Ramos, said of Craven: "Our rugby would not be where it is today if South Africa had not helped us get off the ground in the 1960s. Danie Craven was a great friend to us."

Legends of **RUGBY**

GERALD DAVIES

The epitome of attacking, running rugby, Welsh legend Gerald Davies has gained an army of admirers. Lions captain Willie John McBride likened watching Davies in full flight to "art in motion" and fellow Welsh international Cliff Morgan said of the man: "He wasn't the biggest of men, but he could sidestep, slink past or outspring almost anyone."

And his qualities weren't overlooked by those in the stands either, with commentator Bill McLaren one of his biggest fans. In his book Dream Lions, he wrote: "Davies was a gifted entertainer and often the spark plug to deeds of derring-do by his colleagues in the Cardiff and London Welsh clubs, and on the international scene. Even though he was small in stature, he tackled like the crack of doom and quickly embraced the modern concept of wingers acting as auxiliary full-backs. Frequently, too, he worked in liaison with his Welsh and Lions team-mate JPR Williams to create dazzling switch moves out of defence which left opposing defenders on the wrong foot."

A student of Queen Elizabeth Grammar School in Camarthen, Davies first came into the public eye when helping Loughborough Colleges take the Middlesex Sevens title in 1966. Moving to Cardiff for a teaching job later that year, Davies gained his first call-up for Wales – against the touring Wallabies. Playing in the centre, Davies suffered defeat, as was the case in his next three Internationals. The sequence was broken against England, when Davies ran in a brace of tries – his first on the international stage – in a 34-21 victory. Impressive as the feat was, centre Keith Jarrett overshadowed it with 19 points on his debut.

Nonetheless, after seven caps, Davies had done enough to gain selection for the British & Irish Lions tour to South Africa. Despite having a back injury, Davies still managed nine matches on the tour, including the third Test. Not only did he wow the locals with a 50-yard try against Boland but he was considered by many to be the most creative Lions back in the one Test he played.

The best, though, was still to come for Davies. Back with Wales, the side was beginning to offer glimpses of their true potential as they stormed to three wins in the 1969 Five Nations but were held 8-8 by France and denied the Grand Slam.

A trip to New Zealand followed and, after defeat in the first Test, it was on the internal flight that tour manager Clive Rowlands asked Davies to take up a berth on the wing. At the time Davies regarded such a move as effectively a demotion, but it was a switch that would ultimately lead to him becoming one of the greatest players of all time.

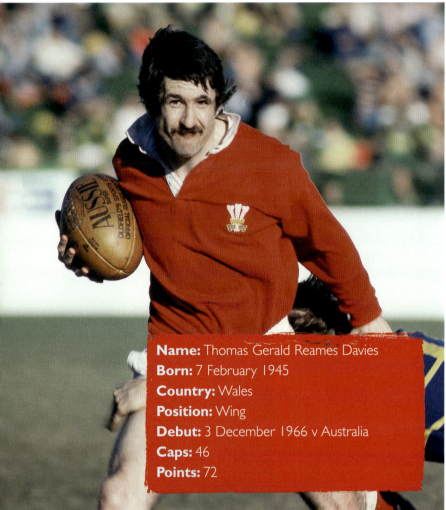

Name: Thomas Gerald Reames Davies
Born: 7 February 1945
Country: Wales
Position: Wing
Debut: 3 December 1966 v Australia
Caps: 46
Points: 72

GERALD DAVIES

FAR LEFT
A Lions legend, Davies was a key member of the 1974 side that won in New Zealand.

BELOW
Davies scores against Ireland at Cardiff Arms Park.

Wales suffered a second defeat to the All Blacks, but the tourists didn't go home empty-handed as Davies scored his third try for Wales in the 19-16 win over Australia in Sydney.

By this time Davies was a student at Cambridge University – where he earned Blues in 1968, 1969 and 1970 – and his studies meant he rested from international duty in 1970.

The break obviously did him good, as 1971 was the most successful in his career. First, Wales took their first Grand Slam since 1952, doing so in breathtaking style and with Davies playing a key role throughout. Their romp to the title almost came undone in only the second game. Scotland had looked to have snatched victory at Murrayfield, before Davies turned on the magic to dash past the bedazzled defenders and touch down in the corner. A kick from John Taylor – dubbed the "greatest conversion since St Paul" – brought Wales a dramatic victory and nothing was now going to stop the Welsh all-stars from clinching the Grand Slam.

The side had timed their run of form to perfection as no sooner had the Five Nations been brought to a close than a Lions side packed with Welshmen (London Welsh alone provided seven) was heading to New Zealand. A narrow 9-3 first-Test win for the tourists was followed by a heavy defeat – although Davies did manage two tries – before the speedster was on hand again with a third Lions Test try to help John Dawes's men into a 2-1 series lead that proved unassailable for the All Blacks.

Davies played in ten of the 26 matches in New Zealand and scored ten tries, including four in one match against Hawke's Bay.

He came back to the UK as a legend. As McLaren wrote: "He returned with his reputation heightened and continued to impress as a wonderfully gifted wing with an elegance and style that was distinctive – pattering steps, the light-footed surge of pace and always with a thought for his colleagues."

Davies was unavailable to tour with the Lions in 1974 (to South Africa) and 1977 (New Zealand), but his achievements on the 1971 expedition were enough to confirm his status as a world great.

Wales' success in the 1970s undoubtedly softened the blow for missing those Lions tours as they played the kind of rugby that is still talked of in reverential tones across the world. To that initial Grand Slam in 1971 they added two further Slams in 1976 and 1978 – the last coming in Davies's final year as an international player.

For his swansong, Davies toured Australia with Wales and captained the side in his 46th and final appearance. It ended in a 19-17 defeat, but Davies scored one more try to take his tally to 20 – level with Gareth Edwards – and make him Wales' joint top try-scorer until Ieuan Evans arrived on the scene some years later.

Davies became a journalist with The Times after his retirement and was awarded a CBE in 2002. He was selected to be on the WRU panel that selected the successor to coach Mike Ruddock, in April 2006.

Legends of **RUGBY**

JOHNATHAN DAVIES

Name: Jonathan Davies
Born: 24 October 1962
Country: Wales
Position: Fly-half
Debut: 20 April 1985 v England
Caps: 32
Points: 81

JOHNATHAN DAVIES

It's hard enough to establish yourself as a legend in one sport, let alone two. But that is what Welshman Jonathan Davies managed to achieve, becoming a star of both rugby union and rugby league. A mercurial outside-half in the mould of predecessors such as Cliff Morgan, Barry John and Phil Bennett, Davies had the ability to dazzle and captivate fans from all over the world, and from both rugby codes.

Born in Trimsaran, Davies made a spectacular entrance to Test rugby, marking his Wales debut against England in 1985 with a try and drop-goal in a 24-15 victory. Along with his prowess with ball in hand, he became something of a drop-goal expert, kicking 13 in Test matches, a record that still stood in 2006.

One of his finest days in union came in the first World Cup in 1987, where Davies guided Wales to third place, still their best-ever finish in the competition. That tournament also saw Davies captain Wales for the first of four occasions, in a pool match against Canada.

Davies, who was made captain of Neath before being transferred to Llanelli, played in six World Cup matches that season, but he saved his best to last, inspiring his side to a 22-21 victory over Australia in the third-place play-off.

That World Cup finish set the ground work for a Triple Crown victory in 1988, Wales' only defeat that season coming against the French, 10-9. Against Scotland, Davies scored one of the finest tries seen at Cardiff Arms Park when, receiving Robert Jones's reverse pass under pressure, he prodded a delicate grubber kick in front of the Scottish back row and beat Derek White to the touchdown.

Little did Davies know it at the time but that Triple Crown was to be his final success in a Wales jersey. After two thumping defeats by New Zealand on Wales' 1988 summer tour, and a humiliating loss to Romania the following December, Davies made the decision to 'go north' and signed a £225,000 deal with rugby league side Widnes.

A procession of union players had moved to league, but few can have made the same impact as Davies, who set records at every turn, playing for Great Britain and starring for Wales in the 1995 Rugby League World Cup.

At Widnes, Davies won virtually every domestic medal in the game and in 1991 he shattered the club's points record for a season with 342. The same year, he was voted First Division Player of the Year by his fellow professionals. Davies was also the fastest player in rugby league history to score 1,000 points.

One of his greatest days in the 13-man code came in a Great Britain shirt when he scored a spectacular try to beat the 1994 Australians at Wembley. It was vintage Davies: first, a dummy to beat the Australia cover, then a searing 50-yard dash to the line that lives long in the memory.

Peter Higham, chairman of Warrington, for whom Davies played for two years, summed up his effect in league: "He's one of the best players ever to have come north – possibly the best. It's a pity he's 33 and not 23. He's a one-off and is going to be difficult to replace."

Warrington coach Brian Johnson added: "The last thing you would want to do is to stifle his creative ideas. Jonathan is one of the unique few who can be

BELOW
Davies runs to score a try against Derek White of Scotland, during the five nations international at Cardiff Arms Park, 1988.

Legends of **RUGBY**

JOHNATHAN DAVIES

considered great players and when you have talent that is well above the norm, it is not always easy to conform to set patterns of play.

"It's not as if he runs around doing crazy things. Sometimes he does things that are contrary to the accepted way of playing, but it is never ridiculous. And when you examine his success rate at creating openings out of nothing, you are not inclined to discourage him."

When rugby union became professional in 1995, it was inevitable that many of those players who had gone to league would return. Davies was the first.

By that time he was 33 and could only be expected to play a cameo role. Although he played five more times for Wales in 1996 and 1997, he was never going to repeat his former glories. He was at least able to go out on a high of sorts; his final match, against England in 1997, saw him share the stage with Will Carling and Rob Andrew, who also played their last Test match that day.

Davies was a maverick throughout his career, and explained his philosophy on the game in The Independent, saying: "What depresses me about many different games these days is the number of players who always take the safety-first option. I don't know if it is the fault of coaches or rigid team plans, but we don't seem to have many players prepared to take a chance

LEFT
Davies was a star in league, here scoring for Great Britain, against Australia, in 1994.

FAR LEFT
Davies holds the Regal Trophy aloft in 1992.

BELOW
Davies came back to Cardiff, after union turned professional, in 1995.

and allow their natural ability to come through. That's what spectators want to see: players trying something different.

"The more unexpected, the more exciting it can be. All right, so you get a slagging-off if it goes wrong but it's still worth doing. Anything you do when the opposition are least expecting it throws them into confusion and when they are confused they are vulnerable."

After his playing career ended, Davies, who was awarded an MBE in 1995, established himself as one of the foremost commentators on the game, working for the BBC as an analyser of both league and union.

Legends of **RUGBY**

LAWRENCE DALLAGLIO

Name: Lawrence Bruno Nero Dallaglio
Born: 10 August 1972
Country: England
Position: No 8/Blindside flanker
Debut: 18 November 1995 v South Africa
Caps: 77
Points: 80

LAWRENCE DALLAGLIO

When Wales fly-half Iestyn Harris was asked to assess the strengths and weaknesses of England's team during the 2003 World Cup, he discovered that much of the good work that team put in revolved around one player – Lawrence Dallaglio. Stop Dallaglio and you stop England was what Harris concluded in 2003, by studying tapes of their matches. The No 8 was the platform for so much of England's best play in the tournament, and so it turned out in the final itself.

Trailing to a try from Lote Tuqiri, it was Dallaglio who set England off on the move that led to Jason Robinson's try and his side's recovery, which ended with a match-winning drop-goal from Jonny Wilkinson. Remarkably, when the final whistle blew in Sydney, Dallaglio had played in every minute of England's 2003 World Cup campaign.

Dallaglio is a natural leader and one of the first things Clive Woodward did when he took over as England coach in 1997 was to make the Wasps player his captain, even though he only had 15 caps to his name.

Dallaglio had a tough start to his reign with an autumn series that saw England take on New Zealand (twice), Australia and South Africa in a four-week spell. England emerged with two draws, one each against Australia and New Zealand.

One of the reasons Dallaglio was handed the captaincy was his leading role on the Lions' 2-1 series victory over South Africa the previous summer. Unfortunately, his captaincy lasted just 14 Tests as he resigned in 1999 following accusations about his private life in a British tabloid newspaper.

His resignation came soon after one of his worst days in an England shirt, the 32-31 defeat by Wales at Wembley. That cost Dallaglio a Grand Slam, and the captaincy passed to Martin Johnson.

Dallaglio, however, always received the full backing of Woodward and when Johnson retired after the World Cup triumph in 2003, it was Dallaglio who took the helm once again.

His run in the England team coincided with the formation of the most prolific back row in history. Dallaglio combined with Neil Back and Richard Hill, and together they won more caps as a unit than any back row before them.

One of Dallaglio's main rivals for the captain's armband in 2004 was Gloucester's Phil Vickery, who was eager to acknowledge his credentials.

"Anyone who can stand up and say Lawrence isn't a good choice is being a bit of an idiot," Vickery said. "I know that if I was going to war then he would be someone I'd want with me in the trenches."

Johnson was in agreement, adding: "Lawrence is a born leader. If you had a group of blokes stuck in the jungle, he would become a leader of that group. He is a strong, charismatic character who enjoys taking responsibility and thrives on it."

Rob Howley, who played alongside Dallaglio for Wasps and the Lions, is another who recognised the wisdom of appointing Dallaglio in the wake of the 2003 World Cup. "Replacing Johnson was never going to be easy but in picking Lawrence, Clive has taken the pressure off the situation," he said. "If anyone else had been given the job they would have found themselves

BELOW
Dallaglio gets to grips with Sale during the 2006 Guinness Premiership semi-final.

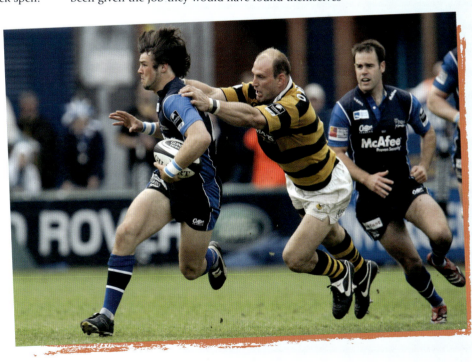

Legends of **RUGBY**

LAWRENCE DALLAGLIO

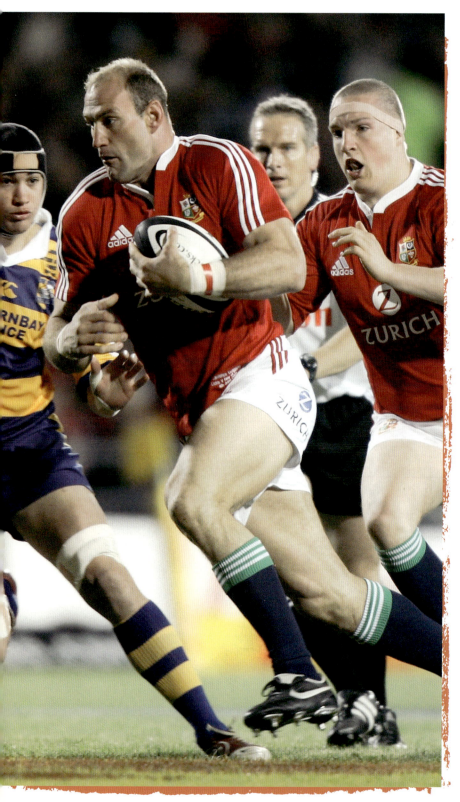

and their record being readily compared to that of Johnson."

A one-club man, Dallaglio signed for Wasps as a teenager and made his debut in September 1993. He was to become an indispensable figurehead of the club, helping Wasps to a succession of domestic and European honours, including the 2006 Powergen Cup.

He was made club captain when Rob Andrew left for Newcastle in 1995 and years later his experience and leadership proved critical on a number of high-profile occasions. In 2004 Wasps lifted the Heineken Cup after beating French giants Toulouse in the final at Twickenham, and a year later Wasps were back at the stadium to clinch their third successive English title.

He won every honour the game has to offer, but his first came in 1993, when he was part of the England team that surprised many by winning the Sevens World Cup. That trophy helped him win his first full England call-up, for the tour to South Africa in 1994.

Dallaglio, who is of Italian descent, went on three Lions tours but in his case it was the best that came first, as he launched himself on the world stage with a series of superb performances as the Lions beat South Africa 2-1 in 1997.

His trips in 2001, to Australia, and 2005, to New Zealand, when the Lions lost both times, were ended by serious injuries. A cruciate knee injury put paid to his tour to Australia and in New Zealand he broke his ankle in the tour opener against Bay of Plenty.

Dallaglio retired from international rugby after England's 2004 tour to New Zealand and Australia, but after regaining his appetite for the Test fray, he announced he would return in the winter of 2005, after successful ankle surgery.

England coach Andy Robinson didn't hesitate in bringing Dallaglio back for the 2006 Six Nations. He resumed his international career when coming off the bench against Wales, and plundered a charging

Legends of **RUGBY**

FAR LEFT
Dallaglio on the charge for the 2005 Lions, against Bay of Plenty.

LEFT
Dallaglio powers towards Gloucester's Ludovic Mercier.

BELOW
Dallaglio, England captain, tackles Roland De Marigney of Italy during the RBS 2004 Six Nations match between Italy and England in Rome, 2004.

trademark try – one of 16 five-pointers he has scored for his country.

In April 2006, Dallaglio signed a two-year extension to his contract at Wasps. By the time he put pen to paper, he had clocked up 285 club appearances, scoring 238 points.

"I'm delighted to have re-signed for the club, which means in effect that I'll finish my playing career where I started, at Wasps," he said.

"This club has always been about offering players the possibility of playing the best rugby they can, maximising their potential and opportunities."

Wasps director of rugby Ian McGeechan said: "Lawrence is one of the giants of the English and world game. He has proved himself an inspirational leader at Wasps over a long period, and combined that with exceptional professionalism in his approach and preparation as a player."

Legends of **RUGBY**

DIEGO DOMINGUEZ

When Italy joined the Six Nations in 2000, it was on the back of hard work from a group of legendary Italian players. At the fulcrum of these efforts was a 5ft 7in fly-half from Argentina, Diego Dominguez.

Dominguez, one of the world's greatest goalkickers, was born in Cordoba and made his international baptism with Argentina, touring with them in 1986. Three years later he won two caps for the Pumas, against Chile and Paraguay.

But with Hugo Porta incumbent in the Argentina No 10 shirt, Dominguez soon moved to play in France, before settling in Milan. In those days players were still able to move from one country to another and he committed himself to the Azzurri, with whom he qualified courtesy of an Italian grandmother.

He was to win 74 caps for his adopted country and his greatest day was that first game for Italy in the Six Nations. The world was watching their entry into rugby's oldest tournament and Italy delivered, with a cherished 34-20 win over Championship holders Scotland. Dominguez not only directed proceedings with calm authority but he kicked six penalties, three drop-goals and a conversion for a 29-point haul.

"It was an historic win, probably the most important in Italian rugby history," Dominguez recalled on scrum.com. "By beating the current holders we've shown we'll be an asset to the Six Nations. It was an important result for the tournament itself too, in that it gives it added credibility."

He knew how important that victory was for rugby in Italy and the supporters who turned out in their thousands to watch that first game.

"We wanted to win for them, and in doing so I think we've put rugby on the map in Italy for some time to come. The Italian public are only interested in sports they excel at, so beating the Scots has given us a certain prestige. I'm sure the Italian public will tune in again in greater numbers for our next game."

Dominguez's first appearance in the Italy shirt had come nine years earlier in a non-cap match against France, and he was thrust into his first World Cup the same year, playing in two more before he finally retired in 2003. You have to say 'finally' in Dominguez's case because he tried to retire on at least two occasions in his record-breaking career. But successive Italy coaches, Brad Johnstone and John Kirwan, convinced Dominguez to change his mind as Italy tried to establish themselves on the world stage.

Johnstone was first to tempt him back, suggesting he would wait until right up to the kick-off if necessary. "I'd give him until five minutes before the match if I had to,"

Name: Diego Dominguez
Born: 25 April 1966
Country: Italy
Position: Fly-half
Debut: 21 April 1991 v Romania
Caps: 74
Points: 983

Legends of **RUGBY**

DIEGO DOMINGUEZ

LEFT
Dominguez was Italy's leading points scorer.

BELOW
The little Italian was also a star of the Stade (Paris) Francais side.

Johnstone said. "To have him would give us a huge boost because we don't have another player of his ability."

Kirwan was of like mind: "Dominguez has demonstrated every week that he's one of the best fly-halves in France."

Nigel Starmer-Smith, the former England scrum-half-turned-media commentator, was delighted to see him go back on his initial decision to quit. "Diego's the man who defies the unwritten 'rules' of the modern game. Forget Diego's [Maradona] one-off 'Hand of God', remember rather the other Diego's everlasting Heavenly Boot!" said Starmer-Smith.

"In 2001 he probably knew that his 'retirement' from international rugby last season was a good way of ensuring a clamour for his return to the Italian national squad. He's back, of course. And why not?"

Dominguez missed Italy's first three matches in the 2001 Six Nations, but returned to score 14 out of 19 points against France, 14 out of 19 against Scotland, and 18 out of 23 against Wales.

He made his name through his goalkicking and by June 2006 only Neil Jenkins had scored more Test points. He finished his career with 983 for Italy, which, when added to his 27 for Argentina, made him one of only two players to have passed the 1,000-point mark. Michael Lynagh and Andrew Mehrtens were third and fourth in the list, and perhaps Dominguez's total can be admired more than those great players, because for most of the time he was playing in a losing team.

But Dominguez was far more than just a goalkicker. He was also a supreme organiser and an underrated defender, as former Italy team-mate Marco Rivaro remembers when Dominguez agreed to play in the 1999 World Cup. "I was very relieved when he said he would play on to the next World Cup, he is a genius," he said. "First of all, he is a really great guy, a professional and really serious about his job, but the great thing is that he is so committed in every game.

"He's well known for his kicking but despite his dimensions, as he's very small, he's a great tackler, I think because he does karate. He has this technique when tackling; I've seen him stealing the ball from bigger attackers."

Canadian Mike James, a long-time team-mate at Stade Français, believes Dominguez was the best fly-half in the world. "I played with Gareth Rees for Canada but Diego has so much confidence and skill that he will score with every opportunity," said James.

Dominguez was one of the stars of the early years of the Heineken Cup, joining Stade Français in 1997. He scored a staggering 756 points in 49 Heineken Cup games, his best season coming in 2000-01, when he scored 188 points in nine games as the French side made the final.

He ended his career on a high in 2005, helping Stade Français to win the French Championship for the 12th time when they beat Perpignan 38-20 at Stade de France in front of 80,000 spectators. He was 39.

A year before, Dominguez helped knock Leicester out of the Heineken Cup, booting 16 points and scoring an injury-time try. Afterwards he said: "No dream ever ended as well." The great man couldn't have put it better.

Legends of **RUGBY**

JOHN EALES

Finding tributes about John Eales is perhaps the easiest job around, so glowing was everyone – from team-mates and rivals to mentors and even politicians – about the man they call 'Nobody', as in 'nobody's perfect'. His decade-long international career generated countless column inches, right to the very end when the gangly lock bowed out with a last-gasp 29-26 win over the All Blacks to retain the 2001 Tri-Nations title. Cue the plaudits, beginning with John O'Neill, then chief executive of the Australian Rugby Union.

"There is no more significant player in the history of the game," he said. "We've been fortunate in Australia to have many great players and many great captains, but I think the combination of great player, great captain and great person is pretty unique."

The coaches were equally effusive. "Rugby has a great custodian in John Eales," said Rod Macqueen, who stepped down as Wallabies coach six weeks before Eales retired. "It has been my pleasure to see him develop into a great captain."

"We're grateful for the legacy he's left," agreed Eddie Jones, Macqueen's successor, while John Connolly, Eales's long-time Queensland coach, once quipped: "John Eales would see the good side of Hannibal Lector."

But it wasn't just the rugby public who owed a debt of gratitude. John Howard, the Australian prime minister, reflected the feelings of the nation when he said: "I wish to record my admiration for the magnificent contribution that John Eales has made to the game of rugby, and to Australian and international sport. He has been an inspirational leader, an outstanding and courageous player, and an example to all in the way he has conducted himself on and off the field."

It wasn't just good manners and sportsmanship that put Eales at the top end of rugby's long list of legends, however; as a player, he was exceptional. Playing for the Brothers club, he was called up by Queensland in 1990 and with the retirement of incumbent Bill Campbell made a second-row spot his own – eventually making 112 appearances for the state. The following year, he made his Wallaby debut in a 63-6 cakewalk against Wales in Brisbane, then starred in a 40-15 trouncing of England. His performance prompted All Blacks legend Colin Meads to predict: "He could be anything, and a force at this level for ten years."

What made Eales special was that he combined the traditional skill set of a second-row with the handling and kicking ability of a fly-half. During his international career, he kicked 31 conversions and 34 penalties which, when added to his two tries, gave him 173 Test points – putting him eighth on the all-time Wallaby point-scorer list as they began their 2006 programme.

In the Super 12 with Queensland Reds he was even more prolific, racking up 402 points from six tries, 66

Name: John Anthony Eales
Born: 27 June 1970
Country: Australia
Position: Lock
Debut: 22 July 1991 v Wales
Caps: 86
Points: 173

Legends of **RUGBY**

JOHN EALES

LEFT
Eales takes the field for Australia, against South Africa in 2001.

BELOW
Eales was one of the finest line-out exponents the world has ever seen.

conversions and 80 penalties – a record never bettered by a forward in the competition. Over the years his kicking for the Wallabies secured several tight contests, none more so than the 24-23 win over New Zealand in 2000, when Eales, with his principal goalkicker Stirling Mortlock having been substituted, took responsibility for a stoppage-time penalty kick in the swirling Wellington breeze. The Bledisloe Cup and, effectively, Australia's first Tri-Nations crown hinged on the outcome – and Eales coolly stroked the ball over from a wide angle.

It was his other talents that had impressed others early in his career, though – notably Rob Andrew, a man he stopped with a crucial try-saving tackle in the 1991 World Cup final at Twickenham. Wallaby coach Bob Dywer mused: "You tell me, how does a 6ft 7in second-rower run down a fleet-footed fly-half like Rob Andrew? As long as I live, I'll never know."

Eales's tackle helped earn Australia their first World Cup and the champions followed it up with their first Bledisloe Cup in 1992, a feat they had failed to achieve since 1986.

A shoulder injury meant Eales sat out 1993, but he was back for Australia's unsuccessful attempt to defend the world crown in 1995. The next year, Greg Smith handed Eales the captaincy. For the first time, things didn't go so smoothly as Australia were hammered 43-6 by New Zealand, losing successive Bledisloe Cup series by 2-0 and 3-0 and also being crushed 61-22 by South Africa (albeit without Eales).

The defeats cost Smith his job and Macqueen took over, so creating a partnership that served as the catalyst for Australia's most trophy-laden era.

A 76-0 destruction of England during Clive Woodward's infamous 'Tour of Hell' in 1998 gave the world some idea of the Wallaby force that was emerging. And they backed up that slaughter with a 3-0 Bledisloe Cup win the same year.

The high point, however, was to come in 1999 when Eales's men romped through the 1999 World Cup, conceding just one try in six matches. The cup was secured with a 35-12 final win over France, giving Eales his second World Cup winners' medal and Australia a place in the record books as the only side to win the greatest rugby show on earth twice.

Still he wasn't finished. That nerveless kick brought the Bledisloe Cup in 2000 and paved the way for successive Tri-Nations titles. The icing on the cake for Eales's supreme career came in 2001. Nobody had ever led an Australia side to a series victory against the Lions and so it was left to 'Nobody' to do just that. Graham Henry's Lions – complete with Eales's great English rival Martin Johnson – came, saw and were conquered 2-1 by the Wallabies. "That was the last frontier, something no Australian team had managed to achieve," said Eales, who captained Australia a record 55 times.

One more Tri-Nations title later, Eales retired and the New Zealanders celebrated.

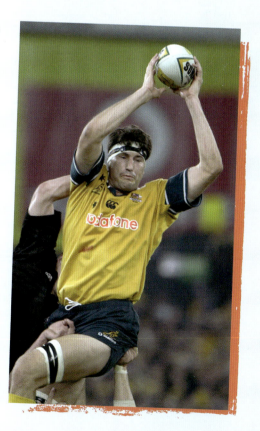

Legends of **RUGBY**

GARETH**EDWARDS**

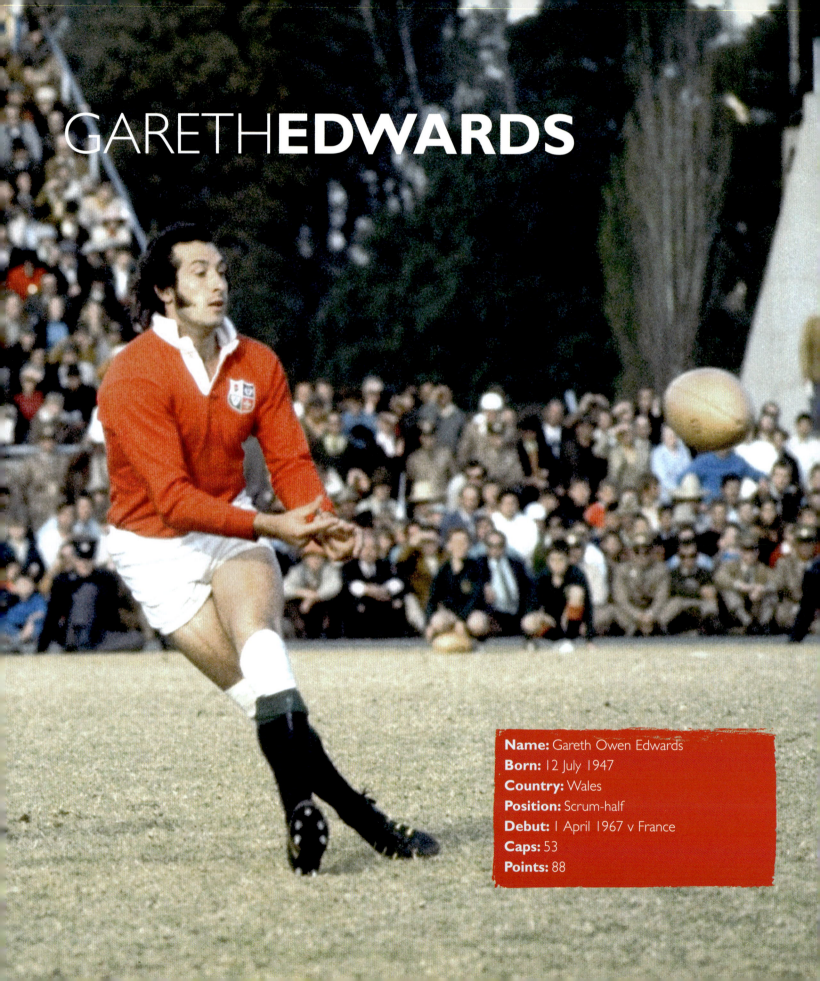

Name: Gareth Owen Edwards
Born: 12 July 1947
Country: Wales
Position: Scrum-half
Debut: 1 April 1967 v France
Caps: 53
Points: 88

GARETH EDWARDS

When Gareth Edwards scored his legendary try against Scotland in 1972, comedian Spike Milligan suggested that a church should be built where he started his run and a cathedral where he finished it, at Cardiff Arms Park. His score and the reaction to it were typical of the way Edwards was revered throughout the rugby world. To most people who saw him play it was simple: Gareth Edwards was the greatest player the world had seen!

On that unforgettable day against Scotland, Edwards, who had already given Wales the lead with a try, burst around the blind side of a scrum inside his own half. He kicked over full-back Arthur Brown and then hacked the ball left-footed into the mud-splattered in-goal area.

Cliff Morgan was in no doubt about Edwards's status. "Of all the players I've seen around the world, he was undoubtedly the greatest," said the former Wales and Lions fly-half. "He could have been a world star in almost any position – scrum-half, fly-half, centre, wing, full-back. He was a genius."

Edwards's try against Scotland was one of 20 he scored in the red of Wales but he scored an even more famous one in 1973 in a Barbarians shirt. Phil Bennett started the move close to his own try-line with a couple of dazzling sidesteps and the ball passed thrillingly through a number of hands before Derek Quinnell fed Edwards, who sprinted up the left flank and dived spectacularly over the line.

Edwards won a then world-record 53 caps for Wales and remarkably those caps – from his debut as a teenager against France in 1967 – were won in consecutive matches over an 11-year period. Edwards was never dropped – the proposition would have been ludicrous!

Edwards only failed to complete one of those games, getting injured in Wales' win over England in 1970 at Twickenham. He was forced off the field with 20 minutes remaining, to be replaced by Chico Hopkins. Maesteg's Hopkins ended up scoring the crucial try, but there was never any doubt Edwards would be on duty for the next game.

Edwards stood like a colossus over arguably the most successful period in the history of Welsh rugby. With Edwards at the helm, Wales won an incredible three Grand Slams, five Triple Crowns, five outright championships and two shared titles, taking the rugby world by storm.

The son of a miner, he became Wales' youngest ever captain, at 20, when he led the side out in 1968 against Scotland and he went on to skipper the side 14 more times.

Even those who saw him in his early teens said he was a genius. Rugby teacher Bill Samuels was the first to spot his potential and was the man Edwards always saw as his mentor. Samuels encouraged him to go to the famous sporting school Millfield, where he was joined by JPR Williams. Attending Millfield allowed Edwards to enjoy a number of sports and his prowess at gymnastics was credited for some of the skill he showed on the rugby field.

Edwards's partnership with Barry John was made in heaven, according to Welsh rugby fans, who saw them play together 23 times. Edwards's superb passing and

BELOW
Edwards after receiving a golden boot at the Painter's Hall, London, for his performance in the Five Nations tournament, 1978.

Legends of **RUGBY**   45

GARETH EDWARDS

tactical understanding gave John the space to rule the roost from outside-half. But Edwards was also a supreme athlete, equally adept at shrugging off forwards to score a short-range try or showing opponents a clean pair of heels with a lung-bursting break. Edwards's fame was also based on his role in another red jersey, that of the British & Irish Lions. Arguments rage about whether the 1971 or 1974 Lions team was the best ever, but to Edwards it hardly matters as he was the ever-present Test scrum-half on both tours.

Before 1971 the Lions were largely a team of glorious sport-ing losers, but the heroics of that summer – the 2-1 Test-series victory, with one draw, and an amazing record in New Zealand of won 22, lost one and drawn one – changed the way that the side was perceived, and Edwards was at the forefront.

John Dawes was Edwards's captain in 1971 and he remembers the great man with affection. "Gareth was the best athlete ever to play rugby football," Dawes says. "He'd never play unless he was in 100% condition and when he was at his peak he was almost unplayable."

Since retiring, Edwards has stayed close to the game as a commentator, as a columnist with the Western Mail and as a director at Cardiff rugby club. He

Legends of **RUGBY**

FAR LEFT
Edwards celebrates a Lions try during the tour of South Africa, in 1974.

LEFT
Gareth Edwards of The Lions is tackled by New Zealand's Alan McNaughton, 1971.

BELOW
Edwards takes on the All Blacks.

has worked for the BBC and S4C, commentating for the latter in Welsh, his mother tongue.

In Who's Who, he lists fishing as one of his hobbies, and even wrote a book on the subject, appearing in the BBC series The Fishing Race.

He also enjoys shooting. In an interview, he once said he loved "putting on a dirty pair of trousers and going fishing or taking a gun into the fields. I do have an ideal place to live, somewhere where I can do my shooting and fishing."

He was awarded an MBE (though, many ask, why not a knighthood?) at the age of just 27, becoming the youngest rugby player to receive such an honour at that time.

Legends of **RUGBY**

IEUAN EVANS

Name: Ieuan Cenydd Evans
Born: 21 March 1964
Country: Wales
Position: Wing
Debut: 7 February 1987 v France
Caps: 72
Points: 157

IEUAN EVANS

In the 1970s, Wales had some of the greatest players the game of rugby has ever seen. But in the 1980s, the fortunes of the men in red dipped and the trophies that had arrived in the era of Gareth Edwards, JPR Williams and Gerald Davies dried up.

One of the few players who prospered even when Wales were losing – the hallmark of a truly great player – was Llanelli and later Bath wing Ieuan Evans.

When he retired from Test rugby in 1998, Evans had won a record-breaking 72 caps for Wales and his tally of 33 Test tries was unsurpassed by any of his compatriots.

Unusually for a wing, Evans was also made captain of Wales. He was given the job for the first time in 1991 against France and kept the armband until the Five Nations match against Ireland in 1995. His run of 28 successive matches as captain was another Welsh record.

These achievements came in an injury-blighted career, and he showed incredible willpower to fight back from a number of setbacks that could have ended his time at the top.

After Evans called it a day with Wales, national coach Kevin Bowring led the tributes, saying: "If it wasn't for the injuries he would have played 102 times, not 72. His absence will leave a big hole in the Welsh squad."

Evans added: "I am 33 years of age and it's very difficult to meet the obligations of both club and country at the moment. It has to come to an end at some point. I've always promised myself I would get out at the top and luckily enough I'm able to do it."

Phil Bennett, a Welsh legend from the era before Evans, was a huge admirer of the Capel Dewi-born flyer. "Ieuan bowed out of international rugby with the sense of timing that has always been his trademark," he said. "He is going out at the top, from where he has graced the Welsh game with skill and dedication for more than a decade. He has been a fabulous ambassador for the sport and his country wherever he has played.

"I think Ieuan has made the right decision. It was obvious that injuries were beginning to wear him down. Luckily, it was not one major injury that has forced him to quit. He has gone out in the right way – in control of the decision."

Evans kicked off his career as a 10-year-old, before turning out for the Carmarthen Quins youth side. Following his education at Queen Elizabeth Grammar School in Carmarthen, Evans moved on to Llanelli at 19 and spent 14 glorious years there. It was at Stradey Park that he made his name, appearing in seven Welsh Cup finals for Llanelli, winning five, and scoring 174 tries in little more than 240 games. One of his most famous tries came against the Wallabies in 1992, as Llanelli beat the tourists 13-9. His exploits at Stradey earned him the nickname The Scarlet Pimpernel, a reference to his long career with the Scarlets and his ability to pop up in the right place at the right time.

In 1985, Evans scored six tries for Wales B against Spain at Bridgend and two years later, in the first of his three World Cups, he bagged four tries in a pool defeat of Canada as Wales went on to finish third.

But Wales were soon to slide from that pinnacle and several players signed for rugby league during some dark days for the nation. The side did have some bright spots, however, winning a Triple Crown in 1988 and, under Evans, the Five Nations title in 1994.

BELOW
Evans powers forward for Wales against Scotland, in 1995.

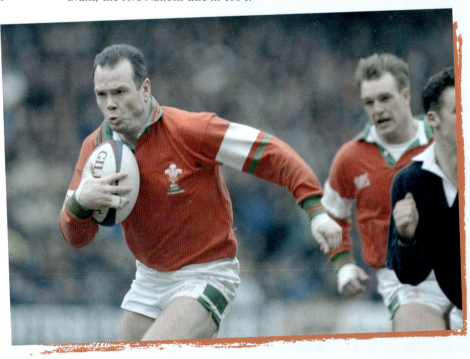

Legends of **RUGBY**

IEUAN EVANS

In the Principality, Evans is best remembered for one particular poacher's try he scored in 1993 at Cardiff Arms Park.

England arrived in Wales seeking their third successive Grand Slam, and having chalked up three successive victories, scoring 83 points, against the Welsh. But with England leading 9-3 and half-time beckoning, Evans struck in historic style. The try stemmed from a kick by Emyr Lewis that seemed to have handed possession back to England. But with Rory Underwood strangely lackadaisical as he turned to field the ball, Evans came steaming up behind him and fly-hacked on. With Underwood powerless to get back, Evans easily outstripped Jon Webb to win the race for the touchdown, allowing Neil Jenkins to convert and hand Wales a 10-9 victory. His place in Welsh folklore was assured.

The victory over England spurred Wales into a Championship victory 12 months later, although it arrived with a tinge of disappointment as they lost the last game of the tournament, to England at Twickenham. Victories over France (24-15), Scotland (29-6) and Ireland (17-15) had proved their credentials, but they fell just short of a Grand Slam.

Evans also holds a special place in the hearts of fans of the British & Irish Lions. In 1989 when the Lions came from behind to beat the Wallabies 2-1, it was Evans who scored the crucial try in the third Test, pouncing on a hopeless pass from David Campese to Greg Martin.

He played an impressive seven Tests for the Lions during three tours, although a groin injury forced him out of the 1997 trip to South Africa prematurely.

The same year he moved across the Severn Bridge to Bath, with whom he won the Heineken Cup in 1998.

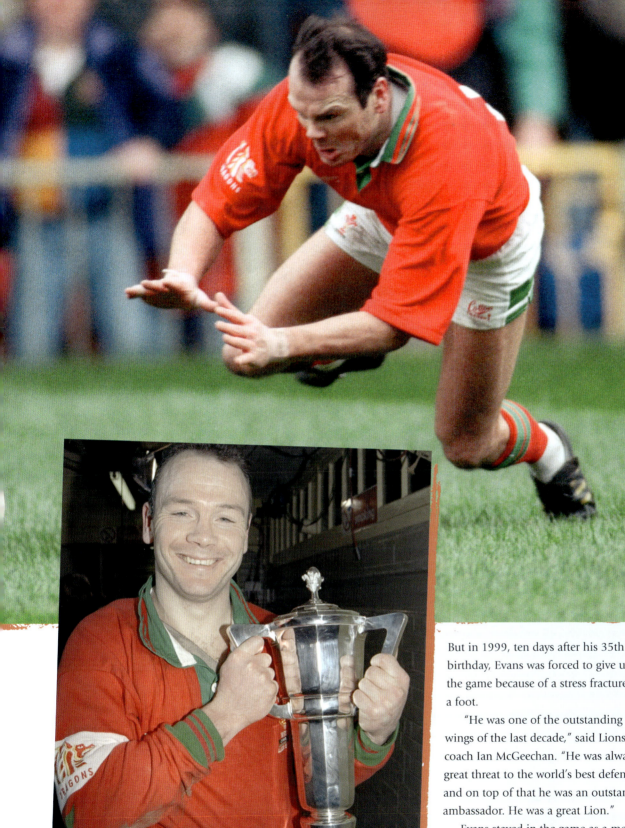

FAR LEFT
Evans of Wales catches the ball during a World Cup match against Western Samoa in 1991.

LEFT
Evans pounces on a loose ball to score for Wales during the Five Nations against England in 1995.

BELOW LEFT
Evans with the Five Nations trophy in 1994.

But in 1999, ten days after his 35th birthday, Evans was forced to give up the game because of a stress fracture in a foot.

"He was one of the outstanding wings of the last decade," said Lions coach Ian McGeechan. "He was always a great threat to the world's best defences and on top of that he was an outstanding ambassador. He was a great Lion."

Evans stayed in the game as a media pundit, his roles including being a columnist for The Sunday Telegraph and a broadcaster for the BBC.

Legends of **RUGBY**

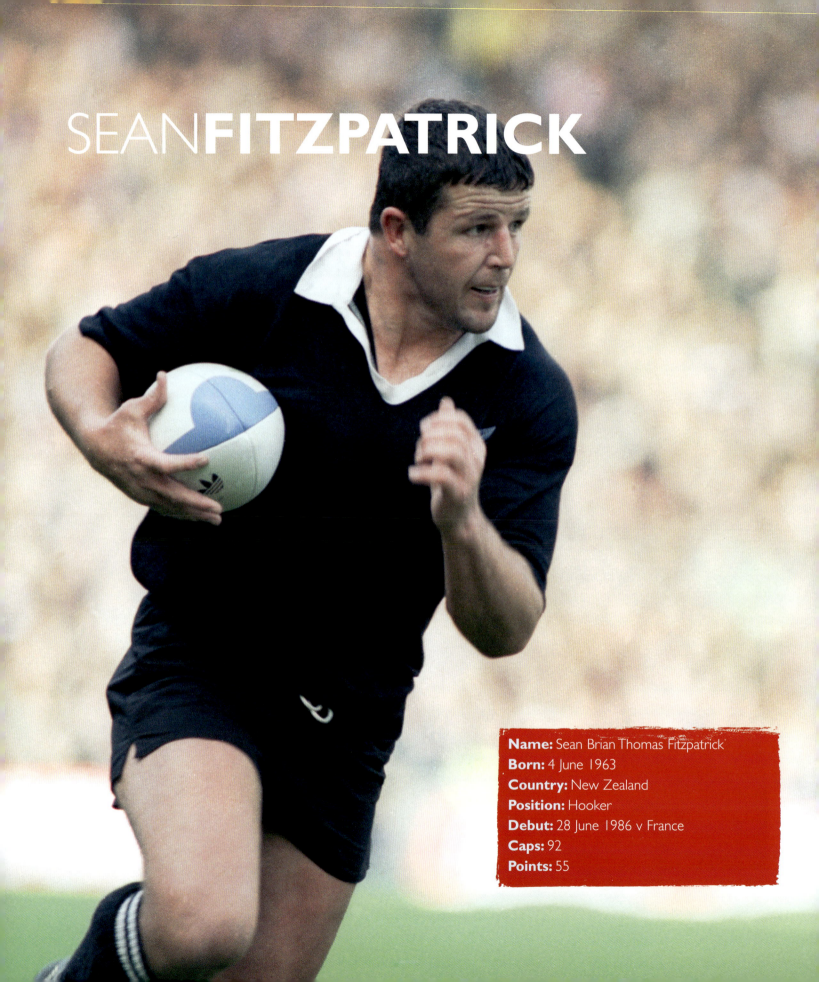

SEAN FITZPATRICK

Name: Sean Brian Thomas Fitzpatrick
Born: 4 June 1963
Country: New Zealand
Position: Hooker
Debut: 28 June 1986 v France
Caps: 92
Points: 55

SEAN FITZPATRICK

During the inaugural World Cup in 1987, an audible groan could be heard across the host nation, New Zealand, when it was announced that captain Andy Dalton had been injured during training early in the tournament. But such was the impact of his young replacement, one Sean Brian Thomas Fitzpatrick, that even though Dalton regained his fitness by the knockout stage, he failed to regain his place.

"When I made my debut in 1986, I was a young kid and just happy to learn from Andy Dalton," Fitzpatrick recalled. "But unfortunately he got injured just before the first game of the World Cup. So I ended up playing all six games and for me it was just incredible to be part of a World Cup-winning side."

That surprise World Cup adventure was part of the most prolific career in All Blacks history. Until his 92-cap record was eclipsed by Jason Leonard, Fitzpatrick was the most capped forward in the history of the game. He is still the most capped hooker.

Fitzpatrick was a natural leader, and a man who commanded the highest respect amongst his rivals and team-mates.

He skippered New Zealand a record 51 times, 41 of which brought victories, and after appearing in that first World Cup, played in the next two as well, reaching the semi-finals in 1991 and then the final in 1995, when he was captain.

His run as skipper coincided with him breaking another record as he played in a remarkable 63 consecutive Test matches, a sequence that was only broken when he was rested, and left on the bench, for a World Cup pool match against Japan in 1995.

Fitzpatrick made his debut as a 23-year-old in 1986, as part of the 'Baby Blacks' side that took on France. The side was so called because the heart of the New Zealand team had been ripped out following the decision of a number of All Blacks to go on a rebel Cavaliers tour of South Africa. That decision led to a number of players being banned, giving Fitzpatrick his chance.

As a record-breaking captain, and despite the fact that New Zealand failed to win a World Cup under his leadership, his qualities were unrivalled, friends and foe alike recognising his special character. He had a number of front-row partners, but the most prolific combination was with Craig Dowd and Olo Brown, the three of them playing 34 Tests together – a New Zealand record.

He was a mobile forward, often giving opponents the feeling that there were four back-row forwards on the pitch, and he was also one of the best lineout throwers in the world. More than anything, though, he possessed a hardness, both physical and mental, that made him an opponent to be feared.

"He had an almost indefinable X factor of which all great All Black captains are made," said Laurie Mains, his coach in the early 1990s. "Following the tour to Australia in 1992 it was obvious he was something special."

A prop in his early days, winning Auckland honours at Under-16 and Under-18 level, he was a slow starter, not making his school first XV until he was in the sixth form. It was current All Blacks coach Graham Henry who moved him to the centre of the front row. "He was apprehensive at first, but I thought he was better equipped to play at hooker," said Henry.

BELOW
Fitzpatrick packs down next to Mark Allen for New Zealand, 1997.

Legends of **RUGBY**

SEAN FITZPATRICK

His father, Brian, was also an All Black, playing 22 Tests between 1951 and 1954.

Many would see the 1987 World Cup victory or the series win over the 1993 Lions as Fitzpatrick's finest hour, but the man himself picks out a victory in 1996, appreciating one of the sport's greatest rivalries.

"In terms of rugby for the purist, for us New Zealanders beating South Africa is always so important," he explained. "We had never won a tour on South African soil, so to do that in 1996 was sensational.

"To see grown All Blacks of 70 or 80 years old crying when we got back and saying, 'Thank you so much for achieving it before I died' was very memorable. That meant a lot to me and being the captain of the team was quite amazing. We don't tour at the moment so it may never happen again."

Not only was Fitzpatrick involved in that historic series win, but in the same year he was a key component of the uckland Blues side that won the first-ever Super 12 competition.

The triumph against the Springboks was a precursor to the first Tri-Nations series, as the game became professional. The All Blacks were to be the first winners.

A year later he was repeating the trick, again lifting the Tri-Nations, Super 12 and Bledisloe Cup trophies before the sun set on his career.

A colossus of the game, Fitzpatrick battled on bravely against injury towards the end of his career, but was forced to admit defeat in 1997, playing his last Test, as a substitute, against Wales at Wembley.

He scored the last of his 12 Test tries – a phenomenal total for a hooker – against

Legends of RUGBY

FAR LEFT
Fitzpatrick raises the Bledisloe Cup aloft after victory against Australia in New Zealand, 1995.

LEFT
Sean Fitzpatrick playing for Auckland Blue feeds the line-out against the Wellington Hurricanes, 1996.

BELOW
Fitzpatrick celebrates New Zealand's World Cup semi-final win over England in 1995, with Ian Jones.

Argentina in 1997, while in 1987 he managed two in one game when New Zealand beat Australia 30-16 at Sydney.

He became the manager of the Auckland Blues for a short time, and was part of the management when they won the Super 12 in 2003. He also worked as a rugby consultant for the New Zealand union, with responsibility for player development.

He was awarded the New Zealand Order of Merit and also managed the New Zealand Colts side in 1999.

Today he works in the media. He has provided expert analysis for ITV, Sky and the BBC, and continues to air his forthright views as a columnist for The Sunday Times in England.

Legends of **RUGBY**

GRANT FOX

Name: Grant James Fox
Born: 6 June 1962
Country: New Zealand
Position: Fly-half
Debut: 26 October 1985 v Argentina
Caps: 46
Points: 645

GRANT FOX

John Wells, the former Leicester coach now working for the RFU, used to say that to create a successful rugby team you needed a tighthead prop, a goalkicker and 13 other players to play around them. Of course he was being glib, but there was more than a grain of truth to his statement, which is one reason why Grant Fox was so highly regarded, for as a goalkicker, the New Zealander arguably had no peers.

There were great goalkickers in rugby before Fox came along in the 1980s, not least the man who inspired him, Welshman Barry John. But Fox redefined the art for a generation, breaking records and establishing some that have stood the test of time.

He needed only six games with the All Blacks to reach 100 points and only 12 Tests, following his debut in 1985, before he overtook Don Clarke's New Zealand points record of 207.

His points totals for the All Blacks (1,067 in 78 games) and Auckland were records, as was his final tally of 645 points in 46 Tests. He was a key figure in Auckland's Ranfurly Shield victory over Canterbury in 1985, which was dubbed, in the Land of the Long White Cloud, the Match of the Century.

But it was at rugby's first World Cup where Fox, a product of Auckland Grammar School, became a legend and where he changed the perception of goalkickers forever.

At that tournament he finished as the leading point-scorer with 126 – an average of 21 per game – as the All Blacks lifted the Webb Ellis Cup on home soil.

It's a record that still stands, and 17 of those points came in the final against France, when he was the lynchpin of a 29-9 victory.

The opening game of that World Cup, against Italy, had been Fox's first home International, his debut having come in Argentina in 1985. And such was his value to New Zealand that he compiled an unbroken run of Tests from 1987 to the second World Cup in 1991.

Fox established his reputation with the Auckland team of the mid-1980s. In Ranfurly Shield campaigns he racked up almost 1,000 points, and in 303 first-class matches he scored a record 4,112 points, 2,746 of those coming in his 189 appearances for Auckland.

Fox's effortless ability with the boot ensured that his tactical talent was often overlooked. He was far more than a goalkicker, although he only scored one try in Test rugby, in the first of a two-Test series against Scotland in 1990. Even then he only dived on the ball when wing Iwan Tukalo kicked nothing but thin air in an attempted fly-hack clear.

Fox's dream of a second World Cup winners' medal ended in the 1991 semi-final, against Australia. Coming into that tournament, the All Blacks, with Fox at the helm, had been close to invincible. And even though Fox's campaign had been affected by a pelvic injury, it says much of the man that he later returned to an All Blacks jersey to play some of the best rugby of his life.

The All Blacks have often been accused of peaking between World Cups and that was the case in the early Nineties, when they defeated the Lions 2-1 just before Fox retired, and then failed to hold their form long enough to win the Webb Ellis Cup in 1995.

BELOW
Fox the commentator, in 1998.

Legends of **RUGBY**

GRANT FOX

But for Fox that titanic Lions series ensured that he finished his international career on a high. He contributed 32 points in those three Tests against the Lions, including a last-minute kick to earn his side a 20-18 victory in the first Test in Christchurch.

After securing the series, Fox, a sports marketing executive, said: "The time has to come when rugby will no longer be the most important thing in my life. I want to go out while I'm at the top of my game.

"Last week was the most intense I've ever experienced in my rugby life. Mentally, it was so tough that you felt almost as if a few years had been lopped off your life."

Shortly after, the 31-year-old Fox decided to opt out of New Zealand's European tour and so he won his final two caps against Australia and Western Samoa in July 1993, saying goodbye with 25 points against the Samoans at Eden Park.

Fox credits Laurie Mains, the All Blacks coach, with giving him a new lease of life following the 1991 World Cup, when he could easily have been jettisoned from the side.

Mains was delighted with his almost flawless kicking game, but challenged him to be a great tactician, and a player who could hurt defences with the ball in hand. Fox revelled in this new-found faith.

"In his way Grant Fox was almost New Zealand rugby," said All Blacks coach Earle Kirton after Fox retired. "He was a great thinker and tactician, and he played some of his best football in the last year and a half. In Test rugby he was probably the best goalkicker the world has seen. Because we don't have another Fox, we have to play a different style of game."

Today Fox is one of New Zealand's most respected commentators and a guest speaker of note, regularly

Legends of RUGBY

FAR LEFT
Fox in the famous colours of Auckland, here against The Lions in 1993.

LEFT
One of the many points Fox scored in international rugby, this time against Wales.

BELOW
And as an assistant coach, back with his beloved Auckland, in 2000.

appearing as a motivator and on the after-dinner circuit. He tried his hand at coaching, with both Auckland and the Auckland Blues. He was with Auckland when they won the NPC in 1999, 2002 and 2003, and after moving to the Blues he finally left coaching to spend more time with his family.

Such is Fox's standing that the All Blacks tried to tempt him out of retirement in 2003, when Graham Henry was putting his national coaching team together. But Fox said: "You never say never but I retired for a reason and those reasons haven't changed."

In November 2005, he was inducted into the International Hall of Fame.

Legends of **RUGBY**

DAVE GALLAHER

"In death, he acquired a mystique. His grave (in a war cemetery in Belgium) became a shrine." So wrote Terry McLean in New Zealand Rugby Legends. In a land full of rugby legends, the Irish-born Gallaher was the forerunner of them all – the captain of the first-ever All Blacks touring side.

Originally from Donegal, he moved with his parents to New Zealand at a young age as part of Vesey Stewart's Ulster Plantation. Initially working farmland in Katikati, Bay of Plenty, his mother was the town's first teacher and the main source of income for a family of ten.

Three years after she died, Gallaher moved to Auckland at the age of 17. It was a decision that would ultimately lead to him becoming a legend, as it was here that he made his name with Ponsonby rugby club.

Winning the Auckland senior championship with Ponsonby in 1897, he played 26 matches for Auckland between 1896 and 1909 – despite missing the best part of two seasons due to his service in the Boer War as a corporal in the Mounted Rifles.

His record of six caps does scant justice to his input into New Zealand rugby. At the beginning of his career, international rugby was at the embryonic stage and Gallaher turned out on six occasions for New Zealand (who hadn't even gained their 'All Black' moniker yet) prior to the country's first-ever International in 1903. Playing the likes of Wellington, New South Wales and Queensland, Gallaher and his team-mates notched up five wins from six games in the build-up to the country's inaugural Test match.

With Australia the opponents, New Zealand won 22-3 in Sydney and the legend was up and running. For his part, Gallaher began as a hooker before taking the controversial position of wing-forward or 'rover' as it was then called.

Great Britain offered the next Test opposition and were duly dispatched 9-3 in Wellington.

Gallaher's greatest achievement came with the first tour to Britain of the 'Originals'. Considering he'd not even been selected for the warm-up tour to Australia, his appointment as captain for the biggest tour in New Zealand rugby's brief history was a shock to many. In fact, so controversial was the decision that on the boat that sailed over he resigned, along with his vice-captain Bill Stead. The vote was put to the players and the pair were reinstated, although not with the kind of majority they'd have hoped for.

Those who had opted for Gallaher and Stead to remain in control were clearly right to do so, as the New Zealanders enjoyed phenomenal success on the

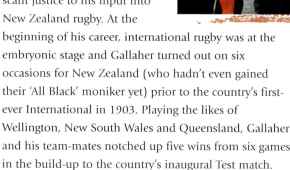

Name: David Gallaher
Born: 30 October 1873
Country: New Zealand
Position: Wing-forward/hooker
Debut: 15 August 1903 v Australia
Caps: 6
Points: 0

DAVE GALLAHER

LEFT
Jerry Collins at a ceremony to officially name the "Dave Gallaher Memorial Park", Co Donegal, 2005.

BELOW
Jonah Lomu pays his respects at the grave site of Dave Gallaher, killed in action in the First World War.

marathon tour. Against the likes of Devon, Cornwall, Gloucester, Oxford University and Bedford, the Kiwis ran in try after try to record cricket-style scorelines.

Before the first Test was even played, Gallaher had already captained his side to 14 wins over various club and regional sides, and the tourists' innovative and dynamic brand of rugby proved too strong for Scotland and England, beaten 12-7 and 15-0 respectively.

It was during the tour that the 'All Blacks' nickname was coined. How it actually came about remains uncertain – one theory is that it was due to a description of them playing like 'all backs', while another centres on the colour of their strip – but either way it was thanks to Gallaher and his team that the New Zealand rugby side gained its famous alias.

Perhaps inevitably, it was the one defeat on New Zealand's pioneering tour that accrued most publicity. The team lost 3-0 to Wales in Cardiff in a game that attained legendary status for the controversial disallowing of a Bob Deans try, which would have squared the match.

The Originals had won 27 successive tour games up to the Wales defeat, and they saw off all subsequent opponents, including Cardiff and Swansea, to complete the British leg of the tour. France provided the next opposition – in what was to be Gallaher's final International – but couldn't get close to the All Blacks as they crumbled 38-8 in Paris.

Two more standard routs of British Columbia followed in North America and the tour was over. Gallaher had captained his side in 26 tour matches – he missed the Ireland Test, won 15-0, due to injury – and they had lost just once. The full tour record was: played 35, won 34, lost one; points for 976, against 59. They scored 243 tries, seven per match, and cruised to victory in nearly all their games.

The position occupied by Gallaher of wing-forward was the cause for much concern to the home sides. He was a big player for the era and his no-nonsense approach to the game provoked criticism from the local hacks, forcing him to respond by saying: "I must confess that the unfair criticism to which I have been subjected, while in Wales especially, has annoyed me."

Retiring from playing following the mammoth tour, Gallaher penned The Complete Rugby Footballer with his vice-captain Stead. That they had the knowledge to create such a book helped to explain why the New Zealanders were so far ahead of the world in a game that was created in the fields of England on the other side of the world.

Individuals were shaping the path of New Zealand rugby and Gallaher was one of them.

He went on to become a selector with Auckland for ten years from 1906 and took on the same role with the national side from 1907 until 1914 and the onset of World War One.

With his age taking him beyond the realms of conscription, Gallaher nonetheless volunteered to serve and he died during action in Belgium, aged 43.

In memory of one of their greats, the Auckland union created the Gallaher Shield, a trophy awarded to the best side within the premier club competition.

Legends of **RUGBY**

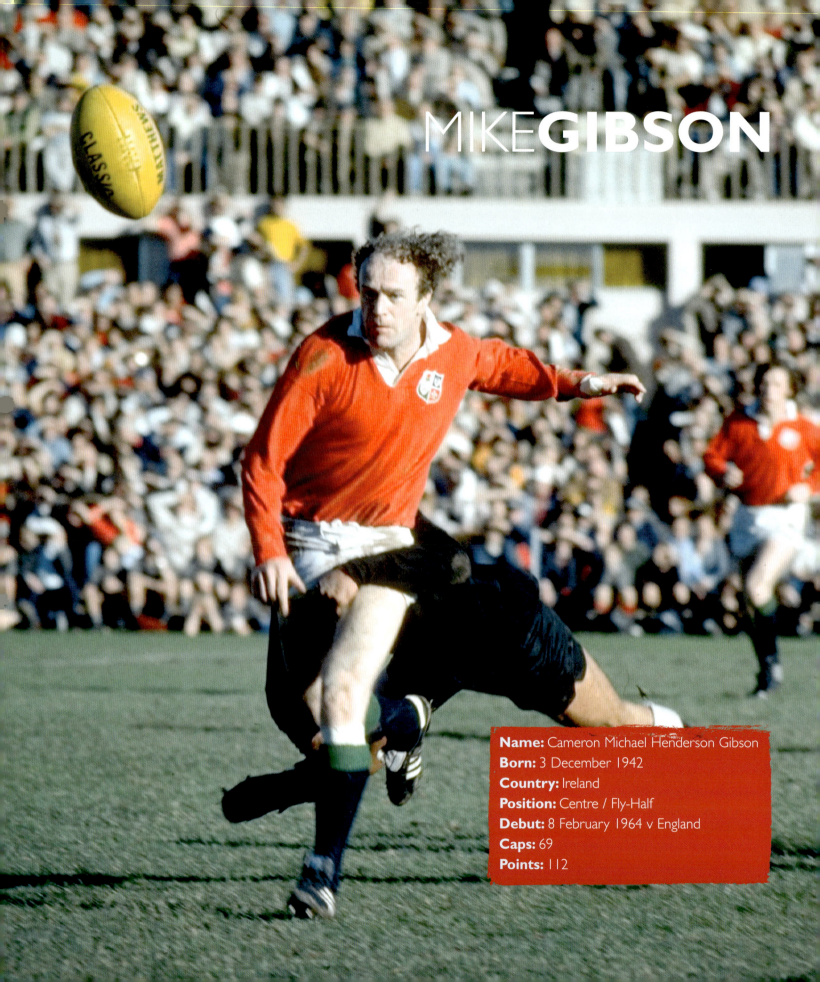

MIKE GIBSON

When John Dawes, captain of the 1971 Lions and coach of some of the great Wales teams of the Seventies, stops to pronounce on a player, then you sit up and take notice. So when Dawes described Mike Gibson, the Irish lawyer from Belfast, as "the complete player", it was high praise indeed. And Dawes, of course, would know, having played with Gibson in the midfield on the 1971 tour to New Zealand, and coached him with the Lions in 1977.

"Mike could run, pass, tackle, kick, you name it," said Dawes. "He had a long career but never played in an outstanding Irish team, so in 1971, among great players, he could show how good he really was. And he did, reaching extraordinary heights."

Gibson, a Cambridge University graduate, was prolific with the Lions, going on five tours in the famous red jersey and being part of the team that rewrote rugby history with a series win in New Zealand in 1971.

And he was no less revered with Ireland, playing 69 Tests for them, in addition to his 12 Tests for the Lions, during a career that spanned 15 years at the highest level.

His 40 caps at centre and 21 at fly-half for Ireland, out of his total of 69, showed his versatility, and it made him the country's most capped player until Leinster's Malcolm O'Kelly went past his famous mark in 2005.

His final Ireland Test came in 1979, when he played a big role in back-to-back victories over the Wallabies at the age of 36. He ended with a win and also started with one, for his debut in 1964 saw Ireland victorious at Twickenham for the first time in 16 years.

Willie Duggan was amazed by Gibson's performance in Gibson's final match in Sydney, as he remembers in David Walmsley's Lions of Ireland. "I wouldn't be a great one for congratulating people on their performances – I've never done that in my life – but the second Test Mike Gibson played for Ireland in Australia in 1979 was absolutely unbelievable," said Duggan.

"You would not believe an individual could do so much. It was the first time I ever crossed the dressing room to shake someone's hand."

Irish Lion Sean Lynch added: "Mike Gibson was the jewel in the Lions' crown; he was just magic. He had everything you could ask for: speed, ability and he knew how to handle a ball. He could dummy-run, scissors, beat a man on the outside or inside, and he could read a game very well, too."

But it was with the Lions that Gibson, who played for Dublin University and Wanderers, earned his worldwide reputation and particularly with the 1971 tour party that returned as rugby immortals.

The first of Gibson's record-breaking Lions tours came in 1966, when Mike Campbell-Lamerton's side suffered a 4-0 whitewash in New Zealand, after going unbeaten in eight games in Australia.

Even then, just two years after his Ireland debut, he was singled out for praise by All Blacks captain Wilson Whineray.

"I believe a team should play to its strengths," said Whineray, after seeing Gibson operate outside Welshman Dai Watkins, "and the Lions' greatest strength was their backs. Their outstanding back was Mike

BELOW
Gibson with his wife Moyra and mother, Mrs Josephine Gibson, after receiving an MBE from the Queen Mother at Buckingham Palace.

Legends of **RUGBY**

MIKE GIBSON

Gibson, who played 19 out of 25 games in New Zealand."

On his second Lions tour in 1968, Gibson showed his versatility and he did it with a record to boot, becoming the first replacement in international rugby. He ended up playing 11 of the 13 matches on tour after Barry John was forced out with injury.

A quicksilver centre for most of his career, Gibson was thrust into the outside-half jersey in 1968, an experience that looked to have stayed with him, and taught him a great deal for the rest of his career.

By the time the next tour came round in 1971, Gibson was in perfect harmony with John and Dawes, as they formed the midfield axis that helped deliver an historic series win, the only one in New Zealand in the history of the Lions.

"It was enriching to play in a side that had so much ability," said Gibson of that experience. "The three midfield men were all of one mind and when Barry had the ball, I tried to think in terms of something seemingly impossible or unorthodox and then got into that position."

The perception of Gibson's influence on the 1971 side has diminished in some quarters through the years, but those close to the trip always acknowledge how crucial he was. Barry Coughlan, the Irish Examiner's rugby correspondent, remembers Gibson's abilities in his book, Irish Lions 1896-2001.

"The general consensus was that Gibson was the man of the tour," said Coughlan, which considering some of the names on the trip was some statement. 'The Complete Footballer' ran a headline in a newspaper following the 47-9 thrashing of Wellington. Gibson's acceleration and deadly changes of direction were the main reason why Wellington were so devastated."

Gibson's fourth Lions tour came in 1974 and because he initially made himself unavailable for selection, only to replace the injured Alan Old towards

Legends of **RUGBY**

FAR LEFT
Gibson on the practice ground, 1966.

LEFT
Mike Gibson of The Lions off-loads to Barry John during the Test Series between New Zealand, 1971.

BELOW
Mike Gibson in for Ireland, 1974.

the end of the trip, he failed to break into the Test side.

Gibson's Lions swansong arrived in 1977 when he made a record-breaking fifth trip with the famous tourists – only Willie John McBride has managed the same number.

Bill McLaren, the legendary Scottish commentator, believes Gibson had it all, from tactical astuteness to wonderful hands and an ability to punt onto a sixpence if he had to. "He's the most complete, all-round footballer I've ever seen," said McLaren. "He had a nose for a score. If there was a score going, you could bet your bottom dollar that CMS Gibson would be on the end of it. Although he looked skinny, he tackled like the crack of doom."

Gibson was awarded an MBE for his services to the game and was inducted into the International Rugby Hall of Fame in 1997.

Legends of **RUGBY**

GEORGE GREGAN

When George Gregan lined up in Marseille for the Test against France on 5 November 2005, his place as one of the immortals in rugby history was guaranteed. On that day, Gregan won his 115th international cap, overtaking Jason Leonard's haul for England, and making him the most capped player for a single country in the history of the game.

"It's been a very enjoyable ride," said Gregan, after passing Leonard's mark. "It doesn't seem so long ago that I was starting my Test career. And I'm still enjoying it, that's the main thing."

Eddie Jones, his national coach at the time, had also worked with him at the Brumbies and knew the player better than almost anyone.

"As captain, George is our foremost leader," said Jones. "He is at the fulcrum of everything we do, a world-class player, a total professional, an outstanding captain. That's why he's so important."

Born in Zambia, Gregan moved to Australia with his family when still a baby, settling in Canberra, a move that was not only fortuitous for the ACT Brumbies but for the whole of Australia. But perhaps we shouldn't be surprised by his record-breaking career as his unusual middle name – Musarurwa – means 'the chosen one'.

In Canberra, Gregan attended St Edmunds College, starting a career that not only spanned the amateur and professional eras but one in which he won every honour the game has to offer: World Cup, Super 12, Tri-Nations, Bledisloe Cup and Test series win over the Lions in 2001.

He has become renowned for his elusive running and bullet-like pass, not to mention his leadership as Wallabies captain, but it was his superb defence that first got him noticed on the international stage. Winning his fourth cap for Australia, he burst on to the Test scene with an astonishing tackle to deny All Black Jeff Wilson in the 1994 Bledisloe Cup clash in Sydney, Wilson spilling the ball as a result and allowing the Wallabies to snatch a 20-16 victory.

Gregan's leadership skills set him apart and in 1997 he was made vice-captain of Australia, having to wait until the great John Eales retired in 2001 to step up to the captaincy itself.

That captaincy took him through the good times and the bad for the Wallabies and in November 2005, when he ran out against Wales, Gregan passed a significant milestone, captaining Australia for the 50th time, second only at the time to Eales, with 55.

"He doesn't need to change anything," explained Wallaby team-mate David Giffin when Gregan took over

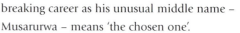

Name: George Musarurwa Gregan
Born: 19 April 1973
Country: Australia
Position: Scrum-half
Debut: 18 June 1994 v Italy
Caps: 127
Points: 99

GEORGE GREGAN

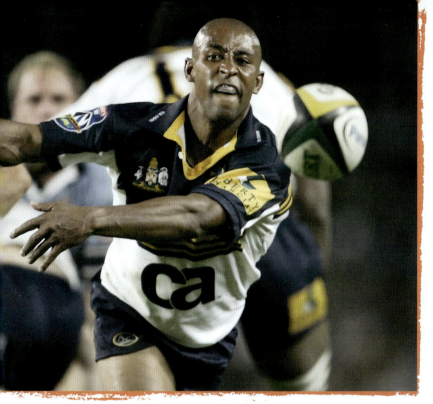

LEFT
Gregan on duty for the ACT Brumbies.

BELOW
With more than 100 caps to his name, Gregan is one of the most famous Wallabies in the history of the game.

But Gregan's humility at the end won him many friends. "It was an epic match," Gregan said. "It was an amazing game to be involved in and I am speaking on behalf of all the Wallaby players and management.

"We put everything into the campaign and came within a whisker of pulling it off. It certainly hurts and always will, but the effort from everyone makes me immensely proud. England deserved the victory and it confirmed what they had shown in the past three seasons.

"I always think that if you are the champion then someone has to come out and prove they are better than you when it counts – England proved this to me."

the captaincy. "His playing position as a scrum-half puts him right in the thick of the action. He has good contact with the forwards and the backs, so that's an ideal place to lead from. George has the advantage of being a good communicator, as I discovered while playing under him at the Brumbies.

"His appointment also speaks volumes of the respect in which he is held by the game's administrators and the rapport that he has with them. Liaising between the team and the administrators is an important part of the skipper's role. The officials have shown their faith in his ability to do that."

In the 12 seasons he has played international rugby, up to 1 June 2006, he has missed just 13 Test matches for Australia. That run included a World Cup winner's medal in 1999, Gregan playing in every match in that tournament bar the pool game against USA, when most of the experienced Wallabies were rested.

Gregan was at his best in the 1999 World Cup. He crossed the try-line twice as Australia moved into the semi-finals with a 24-9 victory over Wales – two of 17 Test tries he has registered, alongside three drop-goals. And in the final against France he featured heavily in both tries as Australia cantered home 35-12.

That World Cup success in 1999 was followed by the agony of defeat four years later, the Wallabies losing to a last-minute drop-goal by England's Jonny Wilkinson.

Gregan has established several commercial interests outside of rugby and has ploughed a great deal of time and energy into raising the awareness of epilepsy, after his son Max was diagnosed with the condition in 2005. With his wife Erica, Gregan has established the George Gregan Foundation, a project aimed at building playgrounds for sick children in hospital. The couple also established a chain of coffee shops in Sydney. Gregan is a national patron for Brainwave and received the Order of Australia for services to rugby in 2004.

In 2006 he started his 11th season with the Brumbies as one of only two foundation players left at the club and the only one to have reached the 100-game milestone. With Gregan only one cap behind Leonard's world record 119-cap haul (five of them gained with the Lions), the Australian is set to end his career out on his own – a fitting tribute to a very special talent.

Legends of **RUGBY**

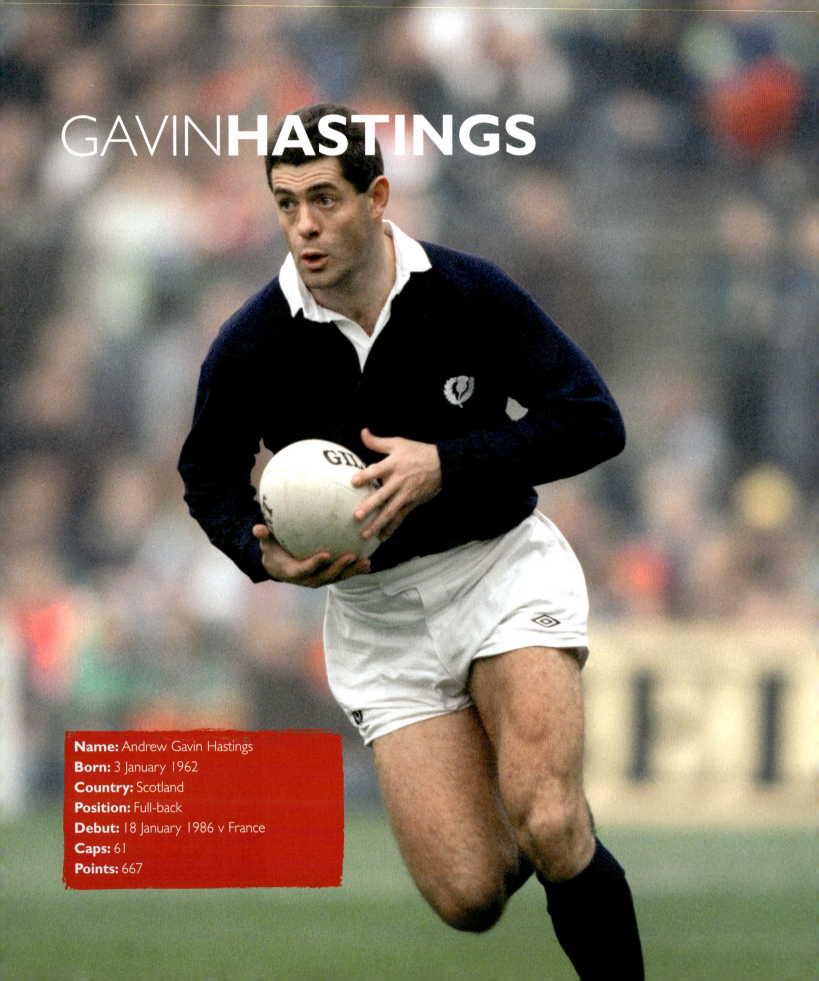

GAVIN **HASTINGS**

Name: Andrew Gavin Hastings
Born: 3 January 1962
Country: Scotland
Position: Full-back
Debut: 18 January 1986 v France
Caps: 61
Points: 667

GAVIN HASTINGS

People should have known something special was about to happen when they saw Gavin Hastings's performance in his first Test for Scotland. The man who had just led Cambridge University into the 1985 Varsity Match was thrown from the student arena into a Five Nations clash with France at Murrayfield. Hastings rose to the occasion magnificently, launching one of the greatest careers in British rugby with six penalties as Scotland prevailed 18-17. He went on to claim a then championship record of 52 points as the Scots shared the title.

Hastings never looked back from that stunning introduction, breaking records and setting new marks across the world. Scotland's leading point-scorer (667) and the man who has kicked more points in the World Cup Finals (227) than anyone else, he was the heartbeat of the Scotland side for almost a decade.

Even before his time at university, or that start against France, he had been earmarked as a future international, captaining the Scotland schoolboys to their first win over England.

Hastings went on to win 61 caps for Scotland – the last 20 of them as captain – as well as winning six caps for the Lions on the 1989 and 1993 tours. On those tours he scored more Test points (66) for the Lions than any other player, but it was the second of the trips, to New Zealand, in which he showed his mettle, courageously ignoring an injured hamstring to captain the Lions to victory in the second Test.

The highlight of his career, however, was Scotland's 1990 Grand Slam triumph, when the Scots sent Murrayfield wild by upsetting favourites England to clinch their second clean sweep in six years.

That Slam was followed by a 21-18 defeat in Auckland, Hastings taking Scotland closer than they've ever been to beating the All Blacks when he kicked two penalties from inside his own half and converted both tries to give Scotland an 18-12 half-time lead.

Captaincy seemed to come easy to Hastings and by the end of his career he had skippered Watsonians, Cambridge University, London Scottish, the Barbarians, Scotland and the Lions.

In Australia in 1989, he and Scott became the first brothers to appear in the same Lions Test team, since Tuan & Jack Jones (Wales) in 1908, and together they managed to turn the vital Test towards the Lions. With the Lions 1-0 down, Gavin scored the try in the second Test that put the tourists in front for the first time with just five minutes left, diving over the line following a pass from Scott. Concussed earlier in the game, he had no recollection of scoring after the match, having to use a television replay to jog his memory.

Four years later Hastings was in magnificent form, but couldn't stop New Zealand turning the tables with a 2-1 series victory themselves. This time he eclipsed his 1989 record with 101 points on the whole tour, 12 of which came in that dramatic second Test when the Lions racked up their biggest ever win over New Zealand, 20-7, in Wellington.

Clem Thomas, in his definitive history of the Lions, summed up Hastings's influence in the famous red shirt, and why coach Ian McGeechan gave him the captaincy

BELOW
Gavin Hastings assists Craig Chalmers of Scotland in a Five Nations match, 1990.

Legends of **RUGBY**

GAVIN HASTINGS

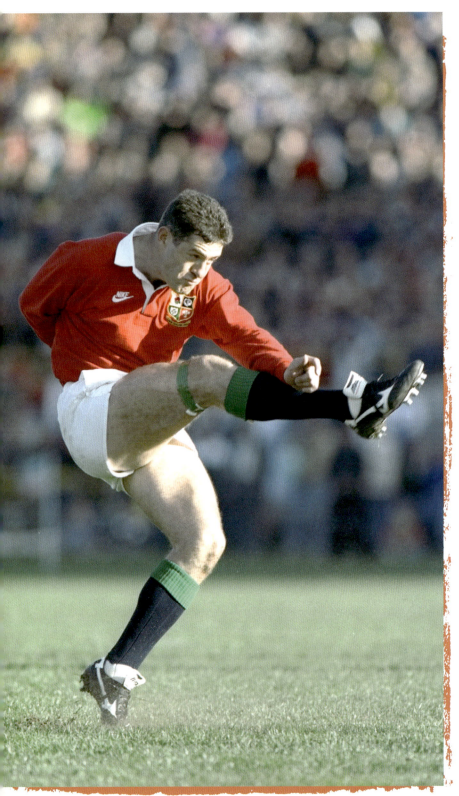

when the pressure back home was on to award it to England's Will Carling, who had led his side to consecutive Grand Slams in 1991 and 1992. "There is no man more respected for his abilities both on and off the field than this delightful Scot, who is the epitome of the rugby man; brave, resolute, adventurous and one who loves a party," wrote Thomas.

The narrow defeat the 1993 Lions suffered reflected well when you consider the 3-0 hammering handed out by the All Blacks when the Lions made their next visit, in 2005.

As skipper, Hastings could do no more, including the individual record of 18 points in a Test, scored in Christchurch, but in a titanic series the Lions came up short. In 1993 he scored more points, 35, in a Lions Test series than anyone had done before him.

In Lions terms he followed an illustrious list of Scottish full-backs that included Andy Irvine and, from an earlier era, greats such as Ken Scotland and Stewart Wilson.

But not everything went to plan for Hastings. In the 1991 World Cup semi-final at Murrayfield, he missed a simple kick with the score at 6-6 – and Rob Andrew then put England through with a drop-goal. Hastings was criticised when he and his team-mates turned up for the final at Twickenham wearing the colours of England's opponents, Australia.

Hastings's World Cup debut in 1987 had started far more brightly, as he scored 27 points against Romania and 19 against Zimbabwe. But a 20-20 draw against France set them up for a quarter-final with hosts New Zealand that was lost 30-3.

He retired after the 1995 World Cup after the Scots were again knocked out in the last eight by New Zealand, this time by 48-30. That game was his 61st and final capped appearance for Scotland, a record that was later surpassed by brother Scott.

Hastings has stayed immersed in sport, helping to manage the Scotland sevens side and establishing

FAR LEFT
As captain of the Lions in 1993.

LEFT
Hastings, in action for his beloved Scotland, at Murrayfield.

BELOW
Gavin Hastings, captain of The Lions tour of 1993 and brother Scott Hastings.

Hastings International, which he set up with Scott. The company has continued with a wide brief and it ensured Hastings was behind projects such as the Scottish Ryder Cup bid, which resulted in Gleneagles being awarded the venue for 2014, as well as consulting on the women's Solheim Cup, which came to Loch Lomond in 2000.

Hastings's full-time move into the business world didn't come until a brief flirtation with American Football, and he helped the Scottish Claymores to victory in the World Bowl at Murrayfield.

His contribution to rugby was recognised with an OBE in the 1994 New Year's Honours List.

Legends of **RUGBY**

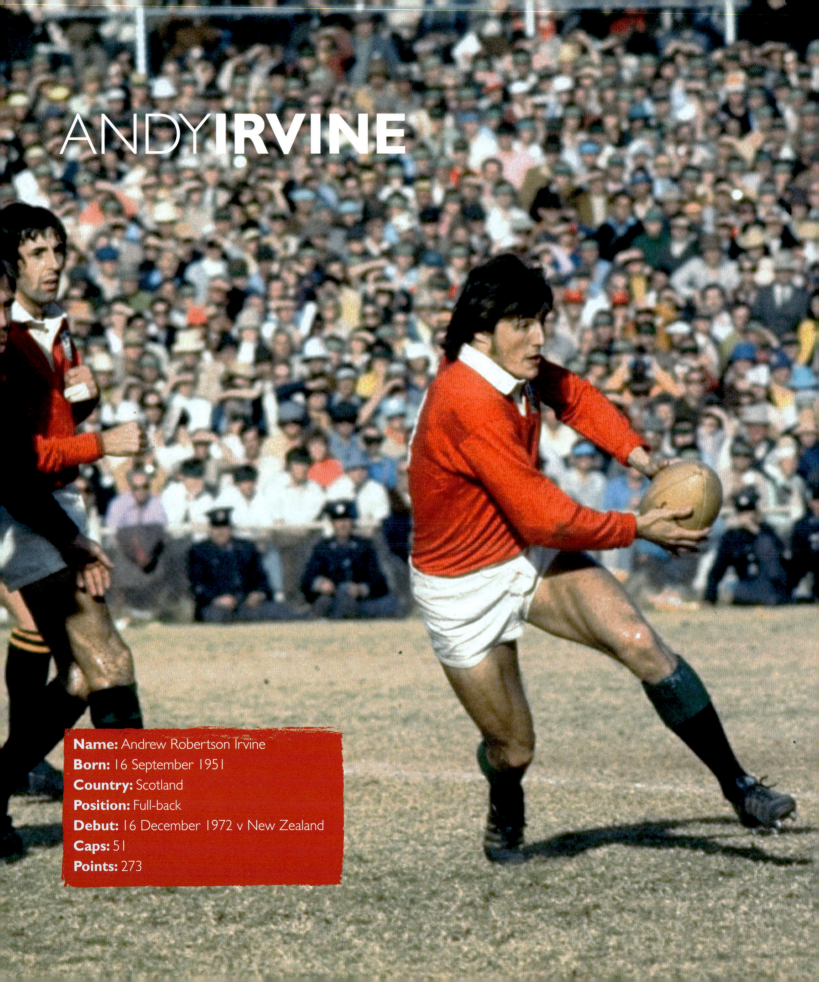

ANDY IRVINE

Name: Andrew Robertson Irvine
Born: 16 September 1951
Country: Scotland
Position: Full-back
Debut: 16 December 1972 v New Zealand
Caps: 51
Points: 273

ANDY IRVINE

Few know the Scottish game better than Bill McLaren and when it came to Andy Irvine, he was more than happy to extol the virtues of this wondrous talent. "He was arguably the most exciting and adventurous full-back in the world game," wrote McLaren. "Whenever he had the ball in his hands, something electric was almost bound to happen and he thrilled crowds from Edinburgh to Cape Town and Hawke's Bay with his pace and weaving running style, quite apart from his outstanding grasp of the game's basic skills. He will always be remembered as a gifted player who had the capacity and the desire to light up the action wherever and whenever he performed."

A relative latecomer to rugby – he didn't play it until the age of 12 – he first found a love for the game when he began studying at George Heriot's School in Edinburgh.

In the modern game, the case for a classic full-back is often questioned as sides deploy wingers in the position so as to make the most of their blistering pace on the counter-attack; Irvine could be called a forerunner to this trend.

For while he did play at full-back, he could also play on the wing, and he wasn't in the position for his ability to catch the high ball but to create chances and openings from deep – something he could do with the greatest of ease. But while today's back-three players sometimes lack the kicking skills of the connoisseur's full-back, the same couldn't be said of Irvine; during his Test career he kicked 25 conversions and 61 penalties for his country, the most famous being the last-gasp strike from inside his own half to salvage a 9-9 draw against England in 1982. Add in his ten tries and even the basic statistics explain why he was so important to the Scots.

In a list of 20 great rugby players, The Scotsman wrote of him: "He could transform a game as if by magic… Irvine had fantastic speed, with an incredible change of pace and acceleration, and he could beat a defender on either side. More than anything, though, he had an eye for attacking that made him a joy to watch, and such a consistent threat to opposition defences that, in their efforts to cover the Irvine threat, they often left other gaps for the Scots to exploit. Such were his gifts that he was a threat even when being denied the ball."

As the latest in a long line of George Heriot's-educated Scottish full-backs, Irvine began his Test career against the mighty All Blacks. His two penalties helped keep Scotland in touch as they slipped to a 14-9 home defeat. Unfortunately for Irvine, he played for Scotland during some lean times. Despite representing his country from 1972 to 1982, the closest he ever got to the Five Nations trophy was a five-way tie in 1973.

But he did have his moments, not least in December 1981 when his 17-point haul of five penalties and a conversion helped Scotland to a stunning 24-15 win over the touring Wallabies. A year later, Irvine helped deliver Scotland's first-ever win in Australia as they humbled the Wallabies 12-7 in Brisbane. That feat was put in context when the Scots lost the second Test 33-9, having put everything they had into winning the opening fixture.

BELOW
Andy Irvine signs autographs for eager Lions fans in 1977.

Legends of **RUGBY**

ANDY IRVINE

From his Scotland days, Irvine saved the best of his Five Nations victories until last. Facing a Wales side unbeaten in Cardiff for 14 years, in 1982 Scotland grabbed their first win in Cardiff for two decades, outscoring the home side by five tries to one, in one of the great championship performances. Irvine captained the side that day – something he did on 15 occasions for his country.

Having another outlet for his talents in the British & Irish Lions gave Irvine a further chance to stretch his rugby muscles. He toured on three occasions, the first of which was in 1974 to South Africa where he played in two Tests on the wing (a 26-9 win and a 13-13 draw), scoring points in both. All told, Irvine played in 13 of the 22 matches played by arguably the greatest Lions side in history, setting what was then a point-scoring record for a Lions tour: his 156 tally comprised five tries, 26 conversions, 27 penalties and a drop-goal.

The second and third tours, to New Zealand and then South Africa, were equally successful for Irvine (though not for the Lions as a whole) as he consolidated his position as one of the game's foremost point machines.

In New Zealand in 1977, Irvine was the deadliest of attackers for the Lions as he took on the hosts' fearsome defences with thrilling panache, even snatching five tries in one game against King Country-Wanganui – a record for a Lions full-back in a representative match. The series was lost 3-1 but Irvine was to have one more go as a Lions tourist before he retired.

FAR LEFT
Irvine the full-back of Scotland attempts a kick at goal.

LEFT
Irvine in action for The Lions in 1977.

BELOW
Andy Irvine of The Lions relaxes after a game in 1980.

Initially not selected for the 1980 trip to South Africa, so beset with injuries were the tourists that Irvine was recalled and made eight appearances, including three Tests. Once again they were defeated 3-1, but Irvine's scoring and playing record was one to be admired – over the course of his Lions career, he appeared in 42 of the 66 games and made nine Tests out of a possible 12. On the points front, he racked up an astonishing 274, including 20 tries.

Adding his 28 Lions Test points to his Scotland tally of 273 made Irvine the first man to score more than 300 points in Test rugby.

As the man who led his country on the pitch, it's fitting that he now leads them off it too as Irvine – the man often voted Scotland's greatest-ever player – is president of the Scottish Rugby Union.

Legends of **RUGBY**

NEIL JENKINS

Name: Neil Roger Jenkins
Born: 8 July 1971
Country: Wales
Position: Fly-half
Debut: 19 January 1991 v England
Caps: 87
Points: 1,049

NEIL JENKINS

In the sport of rugby there have been good goalkickers, great goalkickers and then there's the lad from Church Village in South Wales, Neil Jenkins. Jenks to everyone in the Principality, he became one of the true greats of Welsh rugby through his exploits with the boot.

Affectionately named the Ginger Monster, when he retired from Test rugby in 2002 he was Wales's most capped player and the world-record holder for points scored in Internationals. He scored a mammoth 1,049 points for Wales and a further 41 in four Tests for the British & Irish Lions.

In the 1999 World Cup against Samoa, he passed Michael Lynagh's previous world-record mark of 911 points and he then became the first player in the history of the game to score 1,000 Test points.

Capped at just 19, remarkably he took only 28 Tests to become Wales's leading point-scorer.

Rugby fans seemed to enjoy Jenkins's success later in his career, mainly because of the way he suffered in the early days. As Welsh rugby struggled to live up to the trophy-laden 1970s, Jenkins was made the scapegoat for a struggling side.

But within the game, his true worth was recognised. Lynagh, the man whose record he took, is a big fan. "Neil is more deserving of the record than I am because he has done it the hard way.

"For years he has been part of a Welsh team that struggled, whereas in my career for Australia we rarely had a dip in form," Lynagh said.

"At last he is getting the recognition he deserves as a player. He had to suffer taunts that he is only in the team because of his kicking. Neil is the best goalkicker around, but he would be in the Wales team even if he couldn't land a penalty from 15 yards."

It says much for his mental strength that Jenkins emerged from the dark days with some stunning performances for Wales, and he also produced a series of outstanding games as the Lions beat South Africa in 1997.

On that tour he was switched from outside-half to full-back, to accommodate Gregor Townsend at No 10, and it was his kicking exploits in the midweek side that helped turn the trip in favour of the Lions.

Everyone remembers the way Jeremy Guscott kicked the winning drop-goal in the second Test in Durban to clinch the series 2-0. But it was Jenkins who got them to that point with five penalties to ensure the score was 15-15 before Guscott got the chance to strike.

"I had never felt an atmosphere like the one in Durban before," Jenkins recalled. "When South Africa ran out I thought they were going to run right through the stadium at the other end, they were so up for it. They threw everything at us, but our defence was superb with Dallaglio and Gibbs tackling everything. How we won that match I will never know.

"My first cap against England in Cardiff in 1991 was the proudest sporting day of my life. But my greatest moment on a rugby field has to be playing with the triumphant Lions team in South Africa in 1997, particularly winning the second Test in Durban. Just awesome!"

BELOW
Jenkins was never too far away from an award like this man of the match accolade he won for Cardiff in 2000.

NEIL JENKINS

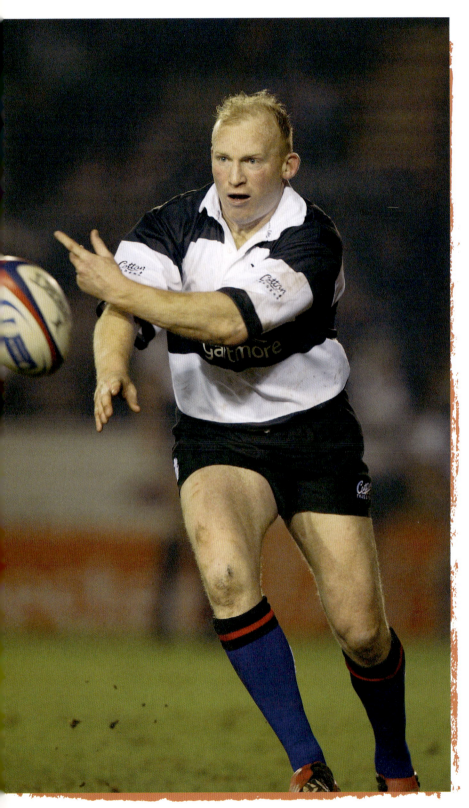

In his autobiography Life at Number 10, Jenkins reveals how he started his working life before rugby became professional, being employed in the South Wales valleys as a scrap merchant prior to ending up as one of the most sought-after players in Britain.

His iconic status at his beloved Pontypridd probably helped him through the bad times with Wales, and he repaid them by helping the club to win the league title and the Principality Cup. He stayed at Pontypridd for 12 years, before moving to Cardiff.

Throughout his career he was a very modest man and it seems as though it was his passion for the Welsh shirt that helped him during the spells when the flak was flying.

"Putting on that red shirt means so much. It is difficult to explain the feeling unless people have actually done it. And for a Welshman the No 10 shirt is particularly special," Jenkins said.

As Welsh rugby changed, so did Jenkins and when many of Pontypridd's players were merged into the new (but now defunct) Celtic Warriors, Jenkins set a remarkable record. He was successful with 44 consecutive kicks for the Warriors, another world record.

"If someone had offered me this career when I was starting out, I would have ripped their arm off to take that and said thanks very much," Jenkins told Rugby World magazine. "I am pretty lucky."

He became an almost permanent fixture in the Wales side after making his debut in 1991 against England, his best moment in a Wales shirt coming eight years later in the same shirt.

Everyone remembers Scott Gibbs's try which 'defeated' England at Wembley in 1999, but Jenkins still had to hold his nerve to kick the conversion. It was actually Jenkins's kick that gave Wales their incredible 32-31 victory.

Legends of **RUGBY**

FAR LEFT
Jenkins was a big supporter of Barbarian rugby, here in 2004, in the famous shirt.

LEFT
Jenkins breaks the world points scoring record during the Rugby World Cup match against Samoa at the Millennium Stadium, 1999.

BELOW
Jenkins was a drop goal expert, kicking three in this game against Scotland in 2001.

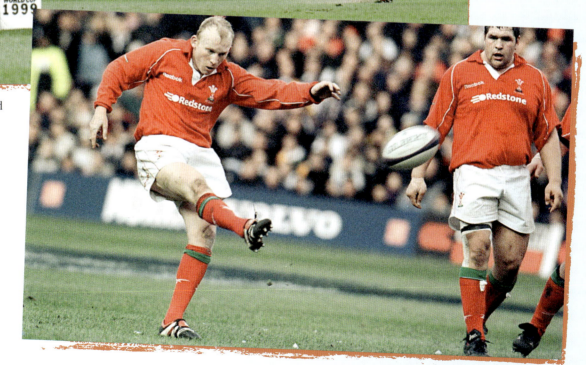

"After Scott Gibbs had scored his try, he just smiled at me, thrust the ball in my hands and said: 'Just kick the damn thing'. After that I was afraid to miss!" Jenkins said. "It was a fantastic day and we haven't beaten England very often in my career – that made it very special."

After retiring, Jenkins started working with the new Wales Academy.

Legends of **RUGBY**

BARRY JOHN

It may seem strange that a player with only 25 caps and 90 points for his country could make the pantheon of rugby legends. But in the case of Barry John the statistics only tell a small part of the story. The George Best of rugby lit up the game in the early 1970s with a scintillating brand of rugby that led to him being considered the greatest talent of his generation.

"The one and only," is how John Dawes describes the Wales and Lions outside-half.

"His reading of the game, his knowledge, taking the right option, kicking off either foot, passing off either hand, gliding through on the break…"

Known simply in Wales as 'The King', John left a nation stunned when he retired in his prime at just 27. He was one of the first rugby players to move in celebrity circles and, according to his autobiography, The King, pressure was the biggest factor behind his departure.

It was in the red of Wales that we first heard the gasps at his skill and the looks of awe from the crowd, but it was in another red shirt where he enjoyed his finest hours – for the British & Irish Lions.

When the Lions arrived in New Zealand in 1971, it was on the back of an awful recent history, and without a series win over the All Blacks in their history. But with John pulling the strings and the side packed with his Welsh colleagues, the Lions won an unforgettable series, 2-1 with one draw, changing the course of rugby in both hemispheres.

"I could always see things early and that enabled me to claim my adversary's space before he knew it," John once said, "and I reckon you can over-analyse videos to the stage where you are frightened to attempt anything.

"Andy Irvine was pretty similar while Besty [George Best] was poetry in motion on a football pitch. Sure, we made plenty of mistakes, but I never worried about them. I was always looking ahead to the next move and working out that if I kept changing my angles of attack, and thinking off the cuff, I'd get more things right than wrong."

John played one Test for the Lions in 1968, but broke his collarbone as they lost to South Africa. It was a different story three years later.

"It wasn't just us who revered him, New Zealand did too," Dawes said after seeing John terrorise the All Blacks in their own backyard.

John played in all four Tests in New Zealand and made an impact that may never be matched. Under the guiding hand of coach Carwyn James, he not only registered a record 191 points in his 17 matches on that

Name: Barry John
Born: 6 January 1945
Country: Wales
Position: Fly-half
Debut: 3 December 1966 v Australia
Caps: 25
Points: 90

Legends of **RUGBY**

BARRY JOHN

LEFT
The King, on form for the 1971 Lions in the fourth Test, in Auckland.

BELOW
John was in his pomp on the 1971 tour, with the Lions.

trip but scored 30 of the Lions' Test total of 48. Of course he had a touch of arrogance, but that is one reason he was loved across the world, and on that tour he taunted his rivals by sitting on the ball in protest at the foul play of Hawke's Bay.

Irish great Mike Gibson remembers John's influence only too well: "He was the name of the 1971 tour. His control of the game and his composure influenced all the other players. His brain operated at a speed that would allow him to do all the things he wanted to do.

"It's not something you would be aware of just viewing the match, but if you experienced playing with him, being in his company, he had a marked influence on players, even on the forwards, who had complete faith in what the back-line was going to do. In the most difficult circumstances he was in control."

No 8 Mervyn Davies saw a different side to John that shows why the No 10 was the coolest customer in the team. "On the Lions tour, we'd all be in the dressing room banging our heads against the wall, but Barry would be in such a relaxed state you'd think he was popping out for a stroll," recalled Davies. "He was so laid-back, he'd just tell us: 'Don't worry, boys, it's only a game. Just give me the ball and I'll win it. It's just the All Blacks; they're not supermen'."

John began his career at Llanelli but later joined Cardiff and linked up in irrepressible style with Gareth Edwards. It was a half-back partnership made in heaven.

John made his debut for Wales against Australia in December 1966, and less than a year later he paired up at Test level with Edwards for the first time, in the 13-6 defeat by New Zealand.

For most people 1971 means the Lions, but in the same year John had already scored a vital try for Wales against France to win the Grand Slam.

Rodney Webb, the man who developed the modern rugby ball, remembers John's incredible skill with the ball in hand. Webb, who also played for England, rates him as the greatest goalkicker of all time and added: "Barry John's punting was phenomenal. He could drop the ball on a sixpence and he could do it every time. He was a genius at reading a game as well, and his goalkicking was so accurate that he didn't just break all the records when the Lions toured in New Zealand in 1971, he smashed them."

John ended his career against France in Cardiff in 1972. He famously declined the chance to kick the final conversion, with Wales already in the clear.

"Rugby is about tries, so I handed the ball to Gareth [Edwards], walked off, kissed my boots and went home," John said. "Statistics didn't matter a damn. Never have, never will. As long as you can put a smile on people's faces, what more could you want?"

John put a smile on the faces of legions of rugby fans. We may have had him in our game for a short time, but the quality he brought will never be forgotten.

Legends of **RUGBY**

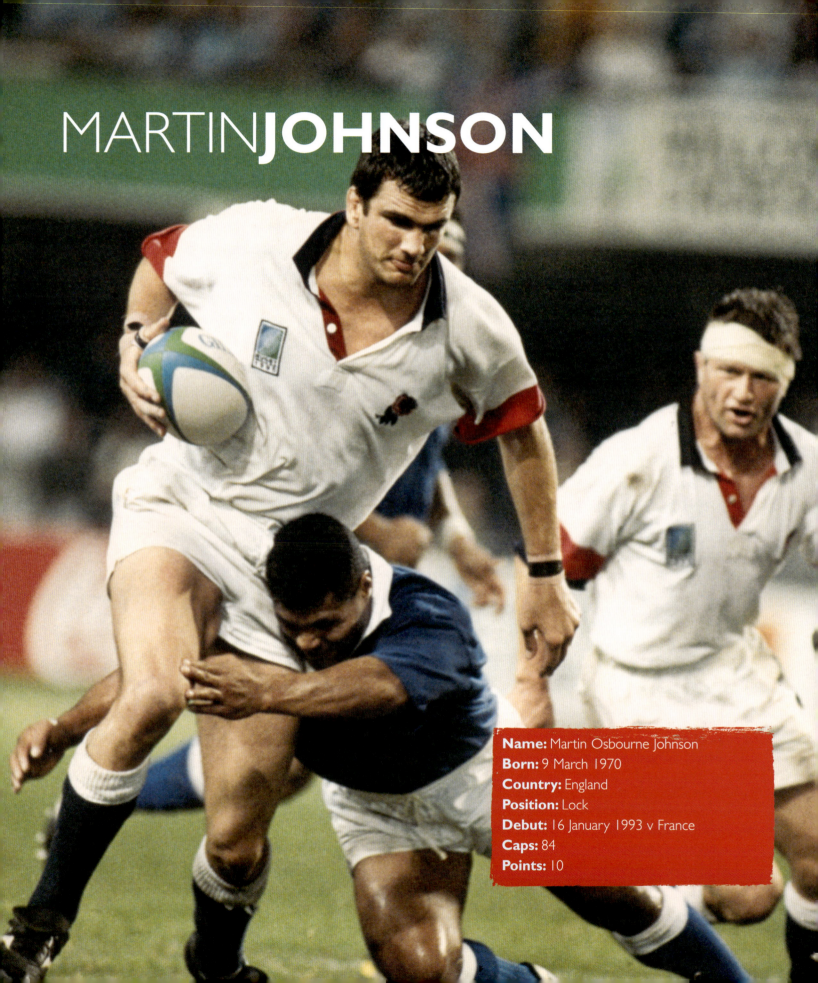

MARTIN JOHNSON

Name: Martin Osbourne Johnson
Born: 9 March 1970
Country: England
Position: Lock
Debut: 16 January 1993 v France
Caps: 84
Points: 10

MARTIN JOHNSON

When England won the World Cup in 2003, it was the right boot of Jonny Wilkinson that delivered the Webb Ellis Cup to Twickenham. But the 20-17 victory over Australia was built on the blood, sweat and toil of every player, and none more so than their inspirational captain, Martin Johnson. So in many ways it was fitting that it was Johnson who took the ball up, gaining the hard yards in the move that led to Wilkinson's famous drop goal.

When he lifted the World Cup to a television audience of millions, it was his last act in an England shirt, as he retired from international rugby shortly after, at the age of 33. Great sportsmen always end on a high.

"You can't overestimate the impact he's had on the game – for club, country and for the British & Irish Lions," said Clive Woodward, the coach who oversaw that World Cup triumph. "Jonno is an awesome individual, a world-class player and his leadership is outstanding."

Former Ireland captain Keith Wood, who played with Johnson on two Lions tours, added: "As a leader he was the best captain I ever had. He would let his body and actions do all the talking. He was the most influential skipper I've encountered and as a player he will go down as one of the all-time greats."

The trophies, accolades and milestones arrived at regular intervals in Johnson's incredible career. He won every honour the game had to offer. When he retired from international rugby, he'd won 84 England caps – 39 of them as captain – and eight Lions caps in an 11-year career. Along the way he collected six Triple Crowns, five championship titles and two Grand Slams (1995 and 2003), as well as playing on three Lions tours, captaining two of them, including the against-the-odds triumph in South Africa in 1997.

In English senior rugby he was a one-club man, and after taking over the Leicester captaincy in 1997 he led them to four successive Premiership titles (1999-2002) and back-to-back European Heineken Cup triumphs in 2001 and 2002, plus a Pilkington Cup victory in 1997.

He also had time for a couple of trips to Buckingham Palace to meet the Queen and pick up both an MBE and a CBE.

He became the first man to captain the Lions on successive tours in 1997 and 2001, and his coach on the first trip, Ian McGeechan, summed up his influence.

"I just thought of him walking down the corridor, and the South Africans opening the changing-room door," said McGeechan. "They'd look up and see Jonno and know that we meant business."

But it so nearly wasn't to be. Johnson joined Leicester in 1989 but not before a year in New Zealand – where he met his wife-to-be Kay – and was selected for the New Zealand Under-21s tour of Australia. Many in New Zealand were desperate for him to stay and change his citizenship. Thankfully for England, he decided to return home after that sojourn.

His England debut followed in 1993 against France and the same year he flew out to replace Wade Dooley on the Lions tour of New Zealand.

LEFT
Johnson holds up The Calcutta Cup after defeating Scotland in the Six Nations match at Twickenham, 2001.

Legends of **RUGBY**

MARTIN JOHNSON

Replacing Johnson at Leicester, England and the Lions was simply not an option. When they built Martin Johnson they broke the mould.

With him out of the England side – along with a few others – England went on a huge downward spiral, finishing well down the table in the three championships following his departure.

His Leicester team-mates were well aware of what they were losing when he packed up his boots. "We know Jonno is probably an impossible guy to replace," admitted his second-row colleague, Ben Kay. Tigers fly-half Andy Goode added: "Losing Jonno's leadership is huge. Not only that, he's the best player in his position in the world and has been for a number of seasons."

Martin Corry replaced him as Leicester captain, and eventually with England. "The important thing is that I don't try to copy Martin," said Corry after this appointment. "Sure, we both lead by example, but I don't have all his attributes, starting with his technical knowledge and captaincy experience."

Leading by example was Johnson's biggest strength, as his England colleague Jason Leonard remembers. "As a captain he would never ask one of his team-mates to do anything he wouldn't. He was a respected figure worldwide, and the complete competitor. He doesn't like to lose at anything and would never take a backward step. He would never avoid hard work – he always rolled up his sleeves and got stuck in."

One of his finest matches came against the All Blacks in June 2003. With Lawrence Dallaglio and Neil Back in the sin-bin, England had to survive four successive scrums on their own line with a six-man pack. Johnson and his fellow forwards did it, enabling England to scrape a 15-13 win of huge psychological significance ahead of that year's World Cup. Asked afterwards what was going through his mind at the

Legends of **RUGBY**

FAR LEFT
Johnson rises highest during a match between Australia and The Lions.

LEFT
Johnson breaks the Australian defence in the 2003 Rugby World Cup Final, 2003.

BELOW
Johnson, the England captain, with the Webb Ellis Trophy, after the team won the World Cup in 2003.

time, Johnson displayed his customary wit: "Nearly my spine."

His final game came fittingly at Twickenham when a Martin Johnson XV beat a Jonah Lomu XV in June 2005. "I'll walk away and won't be doing a George Foreman, although maybe I'll be selling toasters in four years' time!" said Johnson. "That was a brilliant way to go out. I was more emotional than I thought I'd be – I thought I'd just play and walk away. To get a crowd of 42,000 for a match like that is amazing."

In competitive terms, he ended on the losing side as Wasps beat Leicester 39-14 in the Premiership final a month before, his 500th first-class match.

Johnson is still living and breathing sport, raising thousands of pounds for SPARKS, a children's charity founded and supported by top names in sport and entertainment.

Legends of **RUGBY**

MICHAEL JONES

In every generation there are rugby players who transcend the sport and who put back far more than they ever take out… one such man was All Blacks legend Michael Jones. Born in Auckland to a New Zealand father and Samoan mother, Jones made his international debut for Samoa against Wales in Apia in 1986. But his talents were always destined for a higher stage and within a year the dual-qualified flanker got a lucky break when Jock Hobbs, New Zealand's first-choice openside, was concussed shortly before the inaugural World Cup.

Jones stepped in for his All Blacks debut, against Italy, and never looked back. In that tournament opener, he became the first player to score a World Cup try (it followed a penalty try) when he touched down in a 70-6 win over the Azzurri. Remarkably, he was to repeat the trick four years later, scoring the first try of the 1991 World Cup against England at Twickenham.

Nicknamed The Iceman because of his cool demeanour on the pitch, John Hart, the All Blacks coach who first selected him for Auckland, called him "almost the perfect rugby player" and "the greatest rugby player" he had seen.

Jones was inducted into the International Rugby Hall of Fame in 2003 and it says much for his drive and determination that he managed to complete a Master's degree in economic geography at Auckland University during his rugby career.

A deeply religious man, Jones refused to play rugby on a Sunday after making the promise to his dying father. It's a stance he maintains to this day, for, after progressing to coach his beloved Samoa, he takes a step backwards if they have to play on the Sabbath.

Almost any other player would have suffered hugely throughout their career if they had made such a decision, but Jones was no ordinary player. According to The Encyclopedia of New Zealand, when the All Blacks went to Australia in 1988, it was made clear to Mike Brewer that he was only playing in the first Test because the game was on a Sunday, and so Jones was unavailable.

In 1991 such was his standing that the New Zealand selectors took him to the World Cup even though they knew he couldn't play in their third pool match, the quarter-final or the semi-final, as they were all scheduled for Sundays.

Many believe that his stand cost Jones his place at the 1995 World Cup – and, coupled with injuries, it certainly cost him 30 to 40 caps – but once he made that promise he was never going to go back on it.

"When I stopped playing rugby, people soon forgot the player and one thing I'd like to be remembered for is

Name: Michael Niko Jones
Born: 8 April 1965
Country: New Zealand
Position: Flanker
Debut: 22 May 1987 v Italy
Caps: 55
Points: 56

Legends of **RUGBY**

MICHAEL JONES

LEFT
Michael Jones completes a lap of honour held by Xavier Rush and Paul Thomson after he announced he would retire from rugby at the conclusion of the 1999 NPC season.

BELOW
Jones in action for the All Blacks against Italy in 1995.

as the one person who put God before rugby," Jones said. "I feel that people who would never have heard about God have done so because of my stand, because it's brought attention to it. I've been able to show people that there obviously is a God who must exist or else someone wouldn't be prepared to do that."

Jones, who started his rugby career in the backs, was educated in west Auckland, and made a sensational debut for Auckland in 1985 against Canterbury, scoring two tries. From then on he was marked out as a star of the future.

An all-round sportsman, his school rugby coach Owen Stunell described him as an athlete who could have "made it to the top" in other sports, like basketball or cricket, but luckily for rugby he made it his own.

Jones's ability meant he was an automatic choice for the All Blacks and in 1989 he even overcame a horrific knee injury that at one stage was so bad it was feared it could lead to amputation.

The injury slowed him down but after his recovery he emerged in a different part of the back row, now using his guile and analytical rugby brain to rule the roost on the blindside.

Sean Fitzpatrick, the former All Blacks captain, is probably in the best position to judge Jones, having played alongside him for a decade for Auckland and New Zealand. "Michael Jones was the best athlete in my All Black era, superbly conditioned, and had so much ability he could have played in any position," Fitzpatrick concluded. "He went from being the best No 7 in the world to the best No 6."

Jones won a World Cup in 1987 but another highlight was New Zealand's series victory over the 1993 Lions, when he was at the height of his powers.

Jones's playing career ended in 1999, back in the famous Auckland jersey as he helped them lift the NPC title in his 96th game for them. He then committed himself to the Samoan people, becoming assistant coach of the national side and taking up a role at Auckland University, helping the Samoan community. The New Zealand government had asked Jones to chair a consultation group to develop a strategy aimed at helping Pacific youth, and in 2004, when John Boe stood down as Samoa coach, Jones was the only choice to take over.

"I love my country and I'm proud of the fact that we are blessed with special attributes to play rugby," said Jones. "We are a warrior race, suited to a physical contact sport, and I'm very happy and proud to be working with my countrymen. We don't have an army, and we are essentially the force that fights for the honour of our people."

Jones was named the greatest openside flanker of all time by Rugby World magazine and in a millennium poll was voted New Zealand's third greatest player ever, behind Colin Meads and Sean Fitzpatrick. He received a New Zealand Medal in 1990 for service to the Pacific Island community.

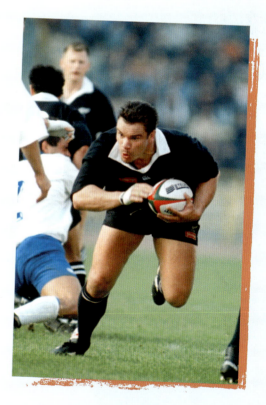

Legends of **RUGBY**

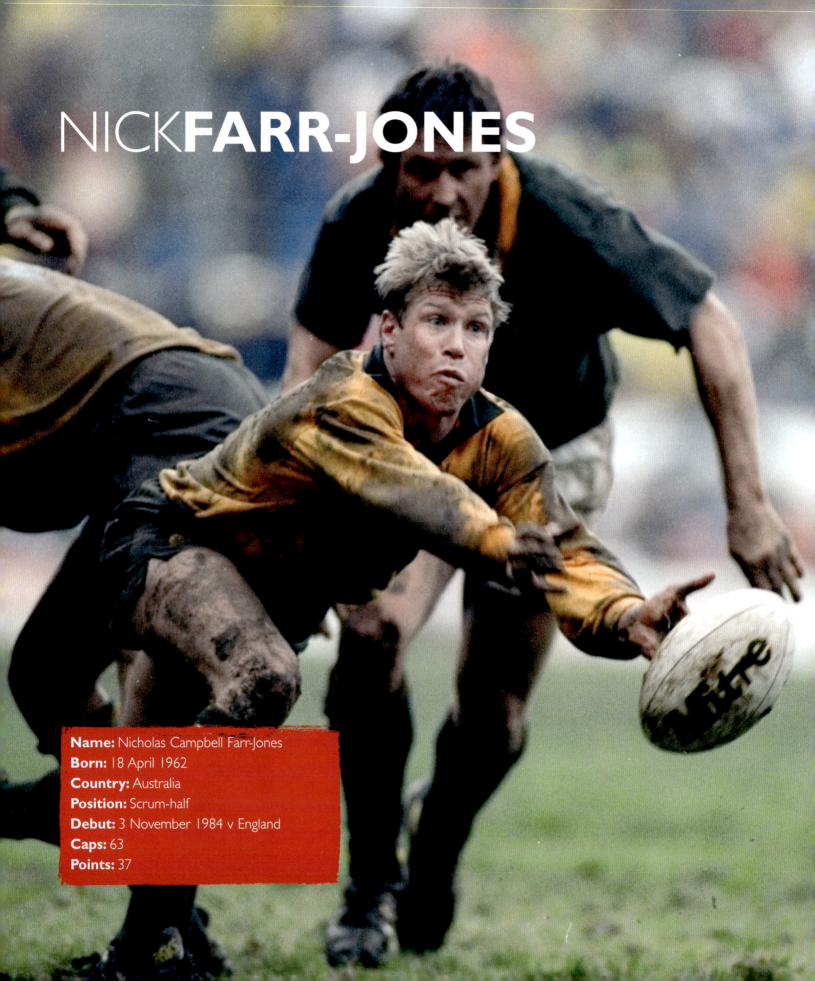

NICK**FARR-JONES**

Name: Nicholas Campbell Farr-Jones
Born: 18 April 1962
Country: Australia
Position: Scrum-half
Debut: 3 November 1984 v England
Caps: 63
Points: 37

NICK FARR-JONES

One of the central figures from Australia's first-ever World Cup triumph, Nick Farr-Jones may have only scored 37 Test points but as a supplier he racked up hundreds. He studied at Newington College and then Sydney University on his way to becoming a lawyer by trade and Australian rugby legend in his spare time. From the Sydney University side he was plucked to play for New South Wales in 1984, and the same year he made his Test debut against England at Twickenham as part of the only Australia team to achieve a Grand Slam on a tour of the home nations.

His debut saw him pair up with Wallaby great Mark Ella at half-back just before his retirement, and allowed him to taste the kind of success that he would grow so accustomed to. The 19-3 stroll against England was followed by wins over Ireland (16-9), Wales (28-9) and Scotland, against whom he scored his first international try in a 37-12 victory at Murrayfield. The 22-year-old's speedy elevation through the ranks wasn't lost on Farr-Jones: "To pull on the gold jersey was something special. I didn't play first XV at school, I didn't play any schoolboy rugby, representative rugby, and to suddenly get on the rocket north because I was playing second division rugby the year before for Sydney University, and to be pulling on a gold jersey the following year, was really out of this world. It's a special feeling of great privilege to be able to represent your country."

Farr-Jones didn't have to wait too long for another significant victory as in 1986 he enjoyed a 2-1 Bledisloe Cup series win over the All Blacks on their patch. It was a significant landmark for the side one year ahead of the inaugural World Cup.

Unfortunately for Farr-Jones, New Zealand were to be first to get their hands on the Webb Ellis Cup, the Wallabies losing out to Wales in the third-place play-off. In their next game, Australia lost out 30-16 to the new world champions in a thrilling Bledisloe Cup battle in Sydney, a failure that cost Andrew Slack the Australian captaincy. The armband was handed to Farr-Jones, still just 25, for the first of his 38 appearances as Wallaby skipper.

A brief honeymoon period saw Farr-Jones's side record two Test victories over England, but the pressure was soon on as the All Blacks were up next and took the series with two convincing wins and a draw.

Farr-Jones's captaincy was put to the ultimate challenge the following year with the arrival of the Lions. The first Test went to plan as the Wallabies cantered home 30-12, but the Lions fought back to take the series 2-1 after a 19-18 nail-biter in the decider in Sydney. The composure that was so evident throughout Farr-Jones's career had been ruffled by Welsh opponent Robert Jones, who trod on Farr-Jones's foot at a scrum in a bid to rattle him, and some questioned his ability to handle pressure. Farr-Jones admitted the series was one of his career low points.

A year on and he was feeling the heat again as the All Blacks took a 2-0 lead in the Bledisloe Cup. With the second World Cup on the horizon, this wasn't the time to be whitewashed by their fiercest rivals. Along with coach Bob Dwyer, Farr-Jones was staring down the barrel, but they managed to pull off a stunning 21-9 win in the final Test.

BELOW
Nick Farr-Jones kicks the ball up-field during the Rugby World Cup final between England and Australia, 1991.

NICK FARR-JONES

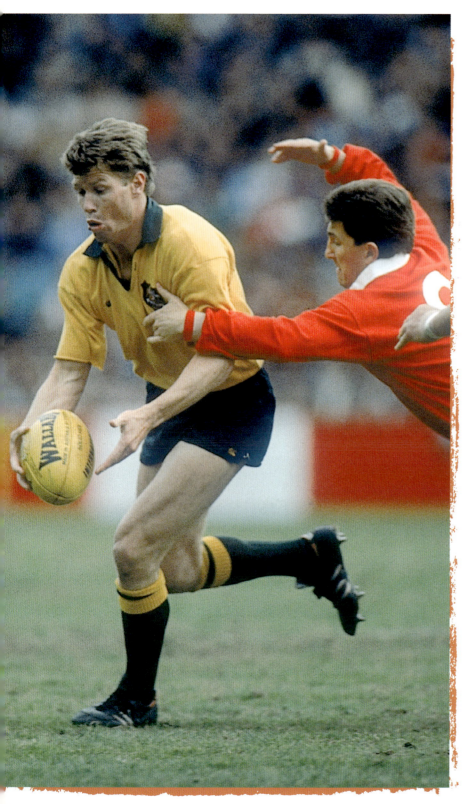

World Cup year arrived and Farr-Jones helped his side to a drawn Test series with the All Blacks, reinforcing the Wallabies' belief that they could beat the best ahead of the main event.

Throughout his career, one of the key factors behind Farr-Jones's success was his partnership with fly-half Michael Lynagh, and they turned out as a partnership in no fewer than 47 Tests. If those two clicked, then so did Australia. "We had a very good relationship, a very good understanding. We are different people but sometimes being different people assists in the way you come together," said Farr-Jones. "One thing I loved about playing with Mike was that I generally knew exactly where he was without him having to call. You might call it telepathy, call it what you want… I knew where Mike was by instinct."

The partnership certainly served Australia well, as Farr-Jones and his troops saw off all-comers at the World Cup. Cruising through the group stages, Australia almost came unstuck in the quarter-final against Ireland and it took a last-gasp try from Lynagh to seal a 19-18 win. The All Blacks gave them less of a fright and were beaten 16-6 to set up a final against England.

England had been expected to play their more pragmatic style of rugby, but instead attempted to play expansively. It cost them the cup as it was Australia, adopting a tighter game, who secured a 12-6 victory.

With this win, Farr-Jones was written into the history books as the first Wallaby to lift the Rugby World Cup.

Legends of **RUGBY**

FAR LEFT
Farr-Jones is tackled by Robert Jones of The Lions during their tour of Australia in 1989.

LEFT
Farr-Jones, captain of Australia passes the ball out from a scrum during a World Cup match against Argentina, 1999.

BELOW
Nick Farr-Jones with the World Cup trophy which Australia won in 1991.

Whereas once they weren't considered fit to be mentioned in the same breath as the South Africans or All Blacks, from this day on the Wallabies were considered one of rugby's 'superpowers'. As a World Cup Champion, Farr-Jones still had no idea of the reception he was about to receive. "I remember being told we had to go on this open-top bus tour and I recall saying, 'What's the point, no one's going to turn up'. But suddenly we were swamped by thousands of people. For months afterwards people were coming up and congratulating me. It was an unbelievable experience."

Farr-Jones's Test career lasted long enough for one more Bledisloe Cup win and a victory against the Springboks before his retirement, although he was persuaded to make a comeback for one last series against South Africa – without the captaincy – in 1993. Australia won and Farr-Jones had finished his career how it had begun, with victory.

Legends of **RUGBY**

DAVID KIRK

Considering he retired from the game at the ripe old age of 26, David Kirk packed an awful lot into his brief, yet glittering, rugby career – not least becoming the first man to lift the Rugby World Cup.

Born in Wellington, Kirk spent his early career with Otago and turned out for the province in 1982, despite coach Laurie Mains doubting his merits as a top-class player.

Dean Kenny was the first-choice scrum-half and they would on occasions work Kirk into the side as a wing or move his rival to fly-half, so as to fit them both in. Kirk's major highlight during his time at Otago was when he played a key role in the South Island's shock win over the North Island in 1982.

From Otago, Kirk moved to Auckland where, under the watchful eye of future All Blacks coach John Hart, he became a regular for the province and played in the side's famous Ranfurly Shield win over Canterbury. Turning out for New Zealand Colts, Kirk gained his first taste of life with the All Blacks as understudy to Andrew Donald on a tour to Britain in 1983, where he sat on the bench for Tests against Scotland and England.

His first full caps came in the summer of 1985 in two Tests against England. Both games were won, 18-13 and 42-15. Australia soon followed and were also defeated, 10-9. A trip to Argentina later that year also brought success for the All Blacks, and Kirk's international career had got off to a flying start, although life was set to get a lot trickier the following year.

The massively controversial rebel New Zealand Cavaliers tour to South Africa in 1986 was to play a pivotal role in Kirk's career. As one of the few All Blacks to turn down the chance to tour the Republic, Kirk gained the Auckland captaincy in the absence of Andy Haden.

Significantly, on the international front, his decision not to tour also paid dividends as he gained the captaincy for a one-off Test against France and a three-Test series against Australia. He won the French match 18-9, but lost the series against Australia 2-1, although he gained some consolation by grabbing a try in the 13-12 win in the second Test.

Upon the return of the rebel tourists, Kirk's place in the starting XV was under pressure but while the captain's armband was duly handed back, he retained his place in the side. Kirk turned out in two more Tests in 1986 in the drawn series with France.

Fate again played a part in Kirk's career in 1987 – World Cup year – when skipper Andy Dalton was

Name: David Edward Kirk
Born: 5 October 1960
Country: New Zealand
Position: Scrum-half
Debut: 1 June 1985 v England
Caps: 17
Points: 24

DAVID KIRK

LEFT
All Black Captain David Kirk goes over for a try during the Rugby World Cup Final, 1987.

BELOW
David Kirk scores for try for New Zealand with the help of teammate John Kirwan (left), 1987.

a dash off the field – in the days when spectators could still run on."

Kirk and his team-mates had achieved something no other rugby side had done – they had become official world champions. As a result, Kirk became the first man to lift the Webb Ellis Cup. "Actually, lifting it was neither a real buzz nor an anticlimax," he said of that historic moment. "There was a touch of melancholy. It must be how people feel at the top of Everest. They only have 20 minutes there and won't ever be back. The only way back is down.

"But that melancholy was overwhelmed by joy. It was all pretty amazing."

Kirk was just 26 years old and the first World Cup-winning captain. Yet the end was near now and he played his last All Blacks match against Australia in July 1987 – just a month after the glorious final. He duly helped deliver the Bledisloe Cup with a thumping 30-16 win.

A hamstring injury gained in that Test forced his international retirement, having already accepted a scholarship at Oxford University – a side for whom he would appear in the Varsity match to earn an Oxford Blue. He won a modest 17 caps, 11 of them as captain, and scored six tries.

Returning to New Zealand in the early 1990s, Kirk coached Wellington from 1993-94 before concentrating solely on his business and media interests.

injured for the first game of the competition against Italy. A young Sean Fitzpatrick took Dalton's place in the side and Kirk took the armband for a second stint.

The biggest rugby journey of Kirk's life had begun and the All Blacks stormed through the opening games, recording a 70-6 win over Italy (in which Kirk grabbed a brace of tries), a 74-13 crushing of Fiji (another try for Kirk) and then a narrower 46-15 victory against Argentina (one more score for Kirk).

The quarter- and semi-finals saw the All Blacks demolish their rivals once more, Scotland (30-3) and Wales (49-6) easily overcome before France provided a slightly sterner test in the final.

Conquerors of Australia in the semis, France found themselves pinned back for much of the game by the tactical kicking of Kirk's half-back partner Grant Fox, and it looked as if their exertions against Australia had left too little in the tank. Along with Fox's 17 points, the All Blacks ran in three tries, courtesy of Kirk, Michael Jones and John Kirwan.

"The game sped by and the French were pretty physical," said Kirk of the 29-9 victory. "But once I scored I had a gut feeling and knew we'd be champions. When the whistle went, there was no massive relief as we knew we were going to win. I just remember making

Legends of **RUGBY**

JACKIE KYLE

Since Ireland joined the Home International Championship – now the Six Nations – in 1883, they have only managed one Grand Slam. In 2006 they came within a victory over France of a clean sweep but, as many times before, the Grand Slam slipped from their grasp.

But in 1948 the Slam was theirs in a period of rugby history where the Irish were pre-eminent. That side had some memorable players, including captain Karl Mullen, but crucially they had a fly-half from heaven, John Wilson Kyle, known throughout the rugby world as Jackie.

Long before Lansdowne Road became the home of Irish rugby, Internationals were regularly held at Ravenhill and 30,000 people packed it to the rafters to see the Grand Slam won with a 6-3 victory over Wales.

Winning a Triple Crown in 1949 and the championship in 1951, to follow the Slam of 1948, ensured this was a golden era for Irish rugby.

Mullen was Kyle's captain in 1948 and he remembers his huge influence over the side.

"We discussed our tactics, and analysis of the Welsh team brought forth the conclusion that they had some great players; mistakes must be cut to a minimum," said Mullen in Ned Van Esbeck's Irish Rugby Scrapbook.

"Indeed, the ability to remain free from error at the crucial moments was a notable characteristic of the Irish side of that period. Then we had Kyle, in my view incomparable before and since. We decided to put our faith in our forwards and leave Kyle to play to our strength. Kyle was the genius and the inspiration… In the closing stages Kyle was magnificent as he sent the Welsh back time after time."

The 1948 Slam produced a number of tributes for Kyle and his team, but none more appealing than the words of Irish rugby journalist Paul MacWeeney, who reconstructed lines from the Scarlet Pimpernel:

They seek him here, they seek him there;
Those Frenchies seek him everywhere;
That paragon of graft and guile;
That dammed elusive Jackie Kyle!

Kyle himself remembers that time with understandable fondness, exposing a few differences from modern-day rugby.

"The first game in 1948 was against France and it was on a Thursday – New Year's Day," he said. "With the game in the French capital, there was great excitement in the team as none of us had been there before.

"It was England next and an 11-10 victory. I was never so glad to hear the final whistle. The final game was something special. Back in my own home town, and

Name: John Wilson Kyle
Born: 10 January 1926
Country: Ireland
Position: Fly-half
Debut: 25 January 1947 v France
Caps: 46
Points: 24

JACKIE KYLE

LEFT
Kyle is chaired off the pitch after winning his 45th cap.

BELOW
Kyle was a Lions legend.

He played in 20 matches on that trip, scoring seven tries and prompting The Rugby Almanack of New Zealand to select him as one of its five Players of the Year. The almanack described him as "an excellent team man, faultless in his handling, able to send out lengthy and accurate passes, and adept at making play for his supports".

The Lions were unlucky to lose that series, drawing the first game 9-9 in Dunedin, where Kyle gave arguably his greatest performance for the tourists. That day he scored three of the Lions points with a try, then put in a famous punt to set up another score for Wales wing Ken Jones.

In John Griffiths's History of the British and Irish Lions, Kyle is remembered as a gentleman who seemed to win as many supporters off the field as he did on it.

"Renowned for his sportsmanship and unsurpassed technical ability, Kyle was portrayed at the time of his international retirement as typifying everything which is cherished in rugby union football," Griffiths said. "Few have subsequently matched his brilliance on the field; off the field, none has shown more gentlemanly or modest demeanour."

That spirit of rugby that coursed through Kyle's veins manifested itself in an incredible way in one nail-biting match against Wales. When Kyle went over in the corner and touched down, the referee awarded the try to trigger celebrations from the crowd and Kyle's team-mates. But once Kyle had picked himself up, he went over to the referee and told him that he had dropped the ball as he went over the line. The referee disallowed the try.

A surgeon by trade, Kyle trained at Queen's University Belfast, and once his rugby career was over he spent more than 30 years working in Africa.

as a 22-year-old student it was really something. I can remember being carried off. It was a real frenzy. Looking back on it now, it was a more remarkable occasion than any of us realised at the time."

Kyle's career was remarkable not just because of his ability; his longevity was something the game hadn't seen before, and when he finally retired in 1958, after an 11-season international career, it was with a then world-record 46 caps.

He had an incredible run in the Ireland team, playing in seven consecutive championship seasons without missing a game before injury removed him temporarily from the scene in 1954. When Ireland played England that season without Kyle in the ranks, it was the first game he had missed since the war.

He made his official Ireland debut against France in 1947, Ireland's first post-war game, and crowds were soon standing in awe of his elusive running and lightning speed off the mark, making him a nightmare for opponents to mark.

Kyle played his final game for Ireland in 1958, going out on a 12-6 win, and only a few weeks after he helped Ireland beat Australia 9-6. He also captained Ireland on six occasions, in 1953 and 1954.

Kyle, who was inducted into the rugby Hall of Fame in 1999, also had an unforgettable Lions tour in 1950, when he played in all six Tests, four against New Zealand and two against Australia.

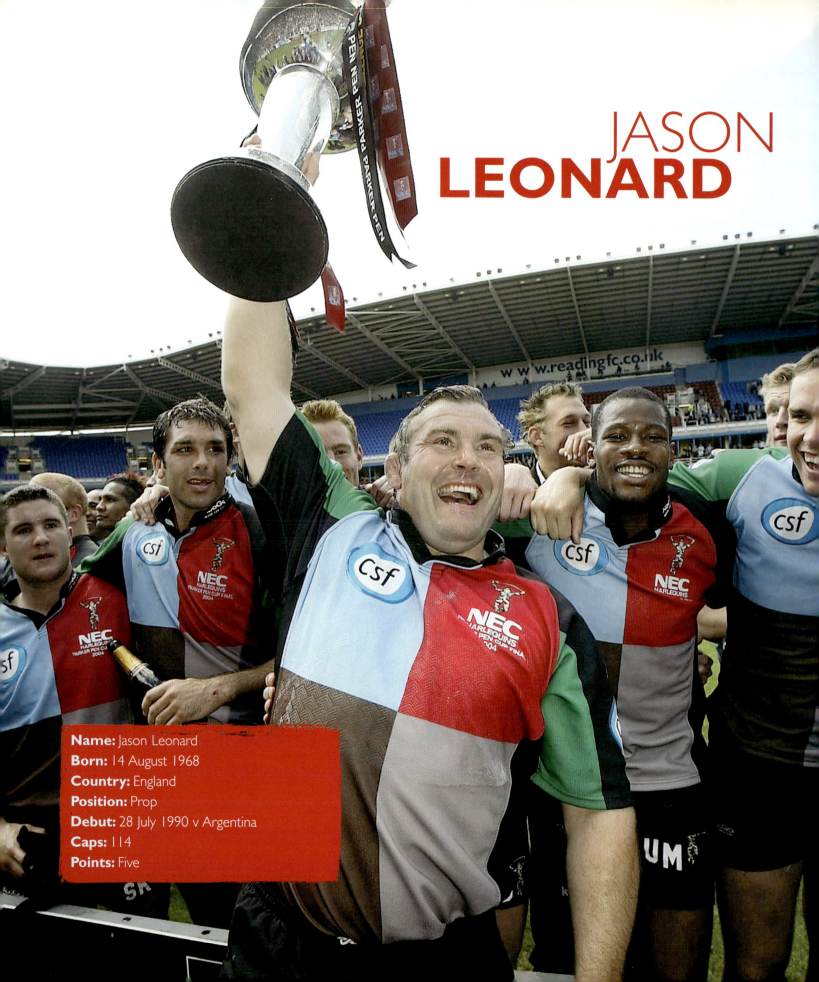

JASON LEONARD

Name: Jason Leonard
Born: 14 August 1968
Country: England
Position: Prop
Debut: 28 July 1990 v Argentina
Caps: 114
Points: Five

JASON LEONARD

When the 2003 World Cup final went into extra time, the only thing that was going to stop England lifting the Webb Ellis Cup was the way they were struggling to cope with referee Andre Watson. England had the upper hand over a weak Australian front row, but Watson was consistently penalising them. So coach Clive Woodward called on the most experienced rugby player in the history of the game, Jason Leonard.

In the semi-final against France, Leonard had passed Philippe Sella's previous world-record haul of 111 caps, but now he was asked to produce his most telling performance. And in the final Leonard immediately placated the irritated Watson and put a stop to the penalties that England were conceding. It was a fitting end to one of the greatest careers rugby has seen and, although he won one more cap in the Six Nations that followed, those who know the game will always view his late intervention in Sydney as his curtain call.

Leonard was the only survivor from the 1991 final, when England had lost to Australia. That 2003 World Cup was Leonard's fourth tournament, and by the end no player had taken part in more matches in World Cup Finals than Leonard's 18.

He had already passed 100 caps earlier in the year and of the five players who had broken the century by the end of the 2006 Six Nations, Leonard is the only one from the unforgiving territory of the front row. It was in 1995 that he became England's most capped prop, in his 38th Test, and a year later he became the youngest England player to win 50 caps when taking the field against Italy at Twickenham.

The World Cup triumph was the pinnacle but before then Leonard had been involved in four Grand Slam sides, in 1991, 1992, 1995 and 2003.

Try-scoring was certainly not his forte, although he did get over the line once, in 1996 during a 20-18 win against Argentina. He was captain that day, and received the honour for a second time in 2003, when England played a World Cup warm-up against Wales.

Leonard started his front-row education at Barking, a carpenter by trade, moving to Saracens and then to Harlequins, but his big break came in 1990. Leonard not only made his Test debut in that year as a 21-year-old but it was in Argentina, where front-row play is an art form. England's selectors knew that if Leonard could cope in Argentina then he could cope anywhere.

And cope he did over an unprecedented career, making a seamless transition from amateur to professionalism and, although he prospered on the field, he never forgot his roots and how to enjoy the spirit of rugby. With nicknames like 'The Fun Bus' and 'The Scourge of the Barking Barmaids', the stories in his autobiography, Jason, were legendary. In that tome he names his 'All-time drinking XV' from team-mates past and present, which sums up his fun-loving character.

He was one of the most popular players ever to grace the sport and this was summed up by his England colleague Jonny Wilkinson. "For any player, let alone a prop, to achieve 100 caps is a massive achievement," Wilkinson said. "All that and he's never missed an opportunity to walk out in an England shirt through

BELOW
Jason Leonard takes on Sebastian Aguirre of Uruguay during the Rugby World Cup match between Uruguay, 2003.

Legends of **RUGBY**

JASON LEONARD

injury. It's a record that is unlikely to be bettered. He is one of the great heroes of the English game. He's renowned as someone who's always welcoming and he's always got a story to tell. It will be a massive blow, both to England and rugby in general, when he finally decides to hang up his boots."

Those boots were hung up in a competitive sense when he came on as substitute in the 2004 Challenge Cup final against Montferrand. At 35, Leonard appeared seven minutes from time after a 14-year, 219-match career. He bowed out in style – with more silverware – as Quins won 27-26.

Leonard was offered a further one-year contract with Quins but said: "I wanted to go out while I'm still playing good rugby. I still love the game and will miss the dressing-room banter and training sessions enormously. Being able to play for my country has been an honour and one I have never taken for granted. And I never did."

In that final season in 2004, then England coach Woodward made one of his few mistakes, failing to recognise that both Leonard and Neil Back had one more Six Nations campaign left in them.

Woodward had already lost Wilkinson to injury and Martin Johnson to retirement. Leonard's final Test appearance came off the bench against Italy in that Six Nations, though he did don an England shirt one more time, in the non-cap 32-12 defeat by the Barbarians in May 2004. He scored a try that day and received a standing ovation from the Twickenham crowd when leaving the field.

It wasn't just in the white of England where Leonard set new benchmarks for props, however, as he went on three successive Lions tours, in 1993, 1997 and 2001.

Leonard's career may have had many highs but it didn't all run smoothly, far from it. He appeared in 40

FAR LEFT
Leonard of the Barbarians applauds the fans prior to the match between England at Twickenham in 2004.

LEFT
Leonard was the world's most-capped player, after the 2003 World Cup.

BELOW
Jason Leonard with his OBE at Buckingham Palace, 2004.

consecutive Tests between 1990 and 1995, an achievement made even more extraordinary because that sequence included an operation, in 1992, to repair ruptured vertebrae in his neck using bone taken from his pelvis. He was told he would never walk again after undergoing life-saving surgery, but in the event the operation hardly made him break stride as he marched towards legendary status.

In 2002 Leonard was awarded an MBE for services to rugby, and an OBE followed in 2003.

Legends of **RUGBY**

BRIAN LOCHORE

As a child, Brian Lochore had his heart set on becoming a jockey. Such was the young Lochore's desire that in order to get his pony to a gymkhana, his father resorted to putting his four-legged friend in the back seat of the family's Chev with its head out of the window!

Once he realised he was going to be too big to be a jockey, Lochore turned his attention to tennis with a huge amount of success – taking the Wairarapa junior title on four occasions and taking on and, in certain instances, beating some of the bigger names in tennis.

When he approached his twenties, however, tennis started to take a back seat to the sport that would make him famous – rugby union – and for a huge chunk of his 20s twenties and early 30s thirties he never even swiped a racquet in anger. Something that, despite his success in rugby, he regrets, as he admitted in Bob Howitt's book New Zealand Rugby Greats. "A shame," he says of the way he stopped playing tennis, "because I think if I had given tennis the time I have rugby, I could probably have achieved a good deal."

Not that he didn't achieve a great deal in rugby. No sooner had it become his sole focus than he was winning recognition across New Zealand.

From Wairarapa College through to Masterton rugby club and then the Wairarapa rep side, Lochore established himself as a No 8 of the highest class. His appearance as a flanker for Wairarapa-Bush against the Lions in 1959 also helped his reputation grow.

As word of Lochore's talent spread, he had All Blacks trials in 1961 and 1963 before eventually making his full debut on the 1963-64 tour to Britain. He played in eight warm-up matches before appearing in the Tests against England and Scotland, winning the first 14-0 but being held to a 0-0 draw in Edinburgh.

By 1965, Lochore had his place at the back of the All Blacks pack nailed down and he started in all four Tests against South Africa. The series ended in a 3-1 victory for the New Zealanders and the next time Lochore took to the field in a black jersey it was as captain of his country. His appointment flummoxed many as the likes of Colin Meads were still in the side, but Lochore proved a hit as a leader – ending up as one of the All Blacks' most successful captains. They lost just three times in 18 Tests during his reign as skipper, all against South Africa at the end of his career.

The 1966 Lions were whitewashed in all four Tests and Lochore also managed to give them a scare with his Wairarapa-Bush team as the tourists squeaked a 9-6 win.

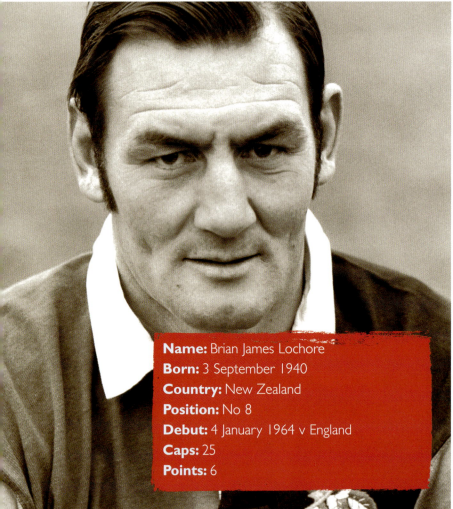

Name: Brian James Lochore
Born: 3 September 1940
Country: New Zealand
Position: No 8
Debut: 4 January 1964 v England
Caps: 25
Points: 6

Legends of **RUGBY**

BRIAN LOCHORE

we saved our bad games for the Tests," said Lochore. "In the Tests we dropped balls we would normally take. It was so frustrating."

The losses tarnished Lochore's impeccable record at the helm. Before the first-Test defeat, he had an unbeaten run that extended for 47 matches.

Lochore chose to bow out following defeat in South Africa and vowed not to make a comeback. It was a vow that didn't last as he returned the next year to face the touring Lions. Unfortunately for him, he again failed to get the ideal send-off as the All Blacks were beaten 13-3 in the third Test in Wellington. While the Lions went on to take the series, Lochore retired again, this time for good.

Lochore's influence on the game didn't end when he left the pitch, however. As a coach he took the unfancied Wairarapa-Bush team into the First Division and he was brought into the international set-up as a selector in 1983. Initially coaching the New Zealand Colts, he was handed the reins to the senior side (along with Alex Wyllie and John Hart) and they duly delivered the first-ever World Cup to the country's rugby-mad public in 1987.

Lochore took on several key positions within the game and in 1999 he became only the second All Black after Wilson Whineray to be knighted. Following Graham Henry's appointment as All Blacks coach in 2004, he accepted a role at the New Zealand Rugby Union as a selector, and today he is playing tennis once again.

LEFT
Lochore, skipper of New Zealand, in action in 1967.

BELOW
Brian Lochore, leads out the All Blacks.

The following season, Lochore led an almighty tour that took them from Canada through Europe and ended with the Barbarians. The All Blacks were never beaten and recorded Test wins over England (23-11), Wales (13-6), France (21-15) and Scotland (14-3). The most memorable contest came in the final match against the Barbarians at Twickenham. With the scores tied at 6-6, Lochore began the move that led to the winning try for Tony Steel.

Lochore's next big challenge came in 1968 against the French, a side he considers one of the best to ever tour New Zealand. Missing the first Test because of a thumb injury, he returned for the second and third winning Tests to secure the series for New Zealand. The matches made a big impression on Lochore.

"France treated New Zealand to glorious rugby," he recalled in New Zealand Rugby Greats. "I doubt that they were appreciated when they got back to France, however. We found after South Africa in 1970 that the Test results count for everything."

In 1970, the year he was awarded an OBE, Lochore made his final appearances as captain in a four-Test series with the Springboks. They lost three of them, managing a solitary win in the second Test in Cape Town. "It's going to bug me for the rest of my life that

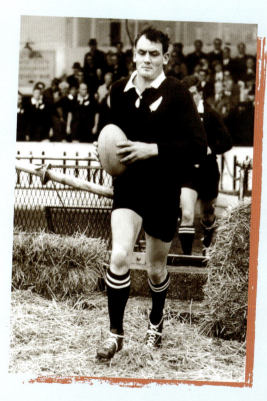

Legends of RUGBY

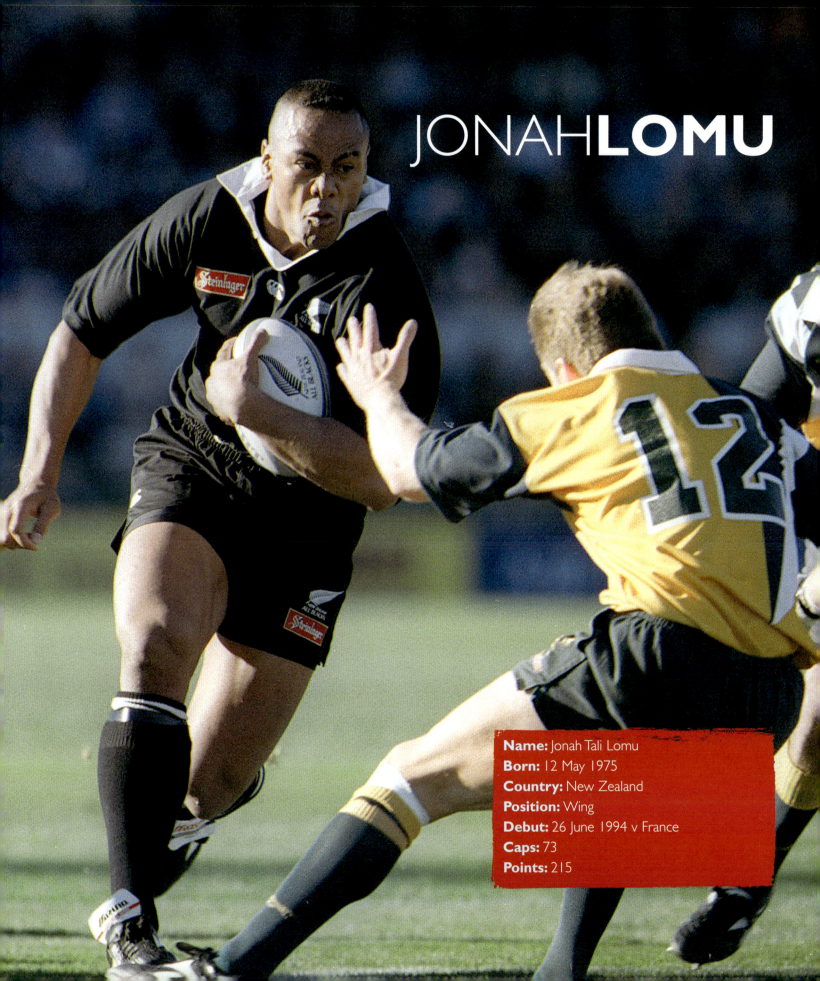

JONAH**LOMU**

Name: Jonah Tali Lomu
Born: 12 May 1975
Country: New Zealand
Position: Wing
Debut: 26 June 1994 v France
Caps: 73
Points: 215

JONAH LOMU

No player has made a bigger impact at a Rugby World Cup than Jonah Lomu. The game's first global superstar, the New Zealander burst onto rugby's greatest stage like a tornado during the third World Cup, in South Africa in 1995. England had arrived at the tournament as Grand Slam champions and one of the favourites for the title. Australia, the holders, had been dispatched in the quarter-finals, so Will Carling and his troops headed to Cape Town confident that they could overcome the All Blacks and take their place in the final for the second tournament running.

But Carling and Co hadn't reckoned on a giant winger who had only celebrated his 20th birthday one month before. Lomu took it upon himself to destroy the European champions with an astonishing four tries, most of them involving going round, through or over helpless Englishmen as if they were mere schoolboys.

His first came within four minutes of the kick-off. From the moment he trampled over full-back Mike Catt on his way to the line, everyone watching knew they were in the presence of greatness. Was this the most natural talent the game had seen?

"Jonah Lomu was the difference – a huge, huge difference," said Carling after England's somewhat flattering 45-29 defeat. "The All Blacks played amazing rugby, but the real difference appeared out on their left wing. We tried to stop him but we couldn't and that's very sad for us. But the man is unbelievable. He's very balanced, has that incredible power and anyone coming onto the ball like he did is almost impossible to stop."

That 1995 World Cup was to end in disappointment for the All Blacks as they succumbed to South Africa in the final, but nobody was in any doubt as to who was the star of the tournament. Lomu had stolen the show and he finished the leading try-scorer with seven tries in five matches.

Four years later it was almost the same story, as Lomu scored another long-range try of power and aggression to help beat England in a pool game at Twickenham. The try sent England into a quarter-final play-off and eventual elimination against South Africa.

New Zealand again failed to lift the Webb Ellis Cup in 1999, this time Australia taking the crown for a second time, but it wasn't for the want of trying on Lomu's part as he once more caused mayhem. The All Blacks crashed out to France in the semi-finals but not before Lomu had scored two tries in which numerous Frenchmen were swatted aside.

At 18st 12lb (120kg) and 6ft 5in (1.96m), Lomu was built for the forwards, but his speed (10.8 seconds for 100 metres) ensured that, to the dismay of international three-quarters everywhere, he ended up on the wing. At school his sprint training included running around the field pulling a lawn-roller with a rope tied around his waist.

The All Blacks were quick to spot Lomu's potential, though in truth it was hard to miss after he announced himself in spectacular style at the 1994 Hong Kong Sevens. Lomu, Eric Rush and Christian Cullen ran amok as New Zealand took the title with a 32-20 win over Australia in the final.

BELOW
Lomu was a star on the Sevens circuit.

Legends of **RUGBY**

JONAH LOMU

His prowess at sevens brought him a gold medal four years later as New Zealand triumphed at the 1998 Commonwealth Games in Kuala Lumpur. Lomu also led New Zealand to victory at the 2001 Sevens World Cup, filling in for the injured Rush.

Once the privileged few had seen him in Hong Kong, it was only a matter of time before Lomu made his New Zealand debut. When that day arrived, against France in June 1994, Lomu was aged 19 years and 45 days – the youngest player to play a Test for the All Blacks.

Born in Auckland of Tongan descent, Lomu grew up in South Auckland and played rugby league up to the age of 14, when his parents sent him to Wesley College, a Methodist boarding school near Auckland.

He first came to the attention of the national selectors when playing for Counties Manukau in the NPC. His promotion followed swiftly, Lomu playing in the Super 12 for the Auckland Blues, Waikato Chiefs and Wellington Hurricanes.

Unfortunately for the game, Lomu was to be struck down in his prime after being diagnosed with nephrotic syndrome, a rare and serious kidney disorder that ultimately led to him having a transplant. The disease first surfaced in 1995, when he took antibiotics in an effort to control it.

John Mayhew, the New Zealand doctor, said in 1997: "The characteristics of this disease, caused by chronic kidney damage, is that he is suffering from low body protein in his blood. How he has managed to train and play I am not sure? We have been monitoring his condition and it has deteriorated markedly in that period of time." Remarkably, two years later Lomu was destroying England in the World Cup.

Eighteen months after his transplant, Lomu made a comeback in Britain, signing for Cardiff Blues in 2005 as he tried to get his career back on track against enormous odds.

FAR LEFT
Jonah Lomu in action for the Cardiff Blues during the Heineken European Cup, 2005.

LEFT
Lomu on his way to demolishing England in the 1995 World Cup semi-final.

BELOW
Jonah Lomu runs onto the field at Twickenham to lead his out his team for The Nobok Challenge Martin Johnson XV versus Jonah Lomu XV match in 2004. Lomu was playing his first international game in three years following a kidney transplant.

Many people believed Lomu would never play again given the severity of his medical condition, and he needed special clearance from the World Anti-Doping Agency, as one of the drugs he was prescribed was on the list of banned substances.

But beat those odds he did and he made his first appearance in a competitive match since his transplant when, in December 2005, he played for Cardiff Blues against Calvisano in Italy.

By the end of the season, he was vowing to fight his way back into New Zealand's squad for the 2007 World Cup. An impossible challenge? Nothing, it seems, is beyond Jonah Lomu.

Legends of **RUGBY**

WILLIE JOHN MCBRIDE

Rarely has one man encapsulated the spirit of something in the way that Willie John McBride did with the British & Irish Lions. In the same way that Gareth Edwards was the ultimate Barbarian thanks to that try, McBride is the ultimate Lion due to his remarkable leadership skills that united four nations to take on and inflict a crushing defeat upon one of the greatest forces in world rugby – the Springboks. Captaining a club side is one thing, captaining an international side is another, but to successfully bring together players from across the United Kingdom and Ireland and take them on a lengthy tour to the other side of the world is a totally different ball game.

Alun Thomas, the tour manager for the 1974 Lions, wrote of McBride: "His outstanding qualities as a player and a man are so well known that I can never adequately describe them in print. He was literally worshipped by the players, not only because of his own courage and strength of commitment, but because they saw in him all the things they would like to be. He shielded them, nurtured them and, above all, inspired them. He shirked nothing, and was that rare breed, a natural leader of men."

A Lions tourist on five occasions, McBride first pulled on the famous red shirt in 1962 when they toured South Africa. The tour was a failure in terms of results – the Lions lost three Tests and drew one – but it did mark the emergence of McBride, as full-back Tom Kiernan acknowledged in the book Lions Of Ireland: "Willie John wasn't expected to get a Test place but he ended up in the team for the last two Tests. He was a relative newcomer to rugby, so he was still immature, but his value in securing possession was pretty high even then."

Having not even touched a rugby ball until his late teens, McBride's rise to the top was phenomenal. He studied at Ballymena Academy, played for Ulster and then gained his first Ireland cap aged just 21 against England in a 16-0 loss at Twickenham.

Unfortunately for McBride, his international career coincided with some lean times with Ireland. In that first year, Ireland finished bottom of the Five Nations and while managing second place on four occasions during his career, they would win the title just once – in 1974. At the peak of his powers and just a few months before the Lions tour that would make him a household name, McBride led Ireland to their first crown in 23 years.

Yet the men in green didn't have the best of starts to the 1974 championship. They lost the opening game 9-6 in France, but grew in stature by recording a 9-9 draw in Dublin against Wales and then defeating England 26-21 and Scotland 9-6.

Name: William James McBride
Born: 6 June 1940
Country: Ireland
Position: Lock
Debut: 10 February 1962 v England
Caps: 63
Points: 4

Legends of **RUGBY**

WILLIE JOHN MCBRIDE

LEFT
McBride earned his world-renowned reputation in the green of Ireland.

BELOW
McBride at the helm of the 1974 Lions.

While his achievements with Ireland were more a case of what might have been – notably in 1972 when Ireland beat France and England in a championship that wasn't completed because of the Troubles – the opposite applied to his career with the Lions, with whom he won a record 17 Test caps.

The 1962 debut in South Africa was followed by the 1966 trip to New Zealand and Australia. They defeated the Wallabies but were whitewashed 4-0 by the All Blacks, McBride appearing in two of the Tests.

It was much the same story in South Africa two years later, only this time they just avoided a whitewash by drawing one Test. It was little consolation to McBride and his team-mates.

Yet the glory days were just around the corner. Inspired by some of the emerging players that would go on to make Wales the dominant force throughout the decade, the 1971 Lions beat New Zealand in two Tests, losing one and drawing the other to claim the only Lions series victory over New Zealand in history.

It was a triumph that has never been eclipsed, but for McBride the next Lions tour was his finest and the one that will forever be mentioned in the same breath as his name.

Unity was the key to McBride's success as a skipper for the Lions. When asked by Welsh fans to get their Lions shirts signed by the Welsh players, he replied: "There are no Welsh players, no Irish players, no Scottish players, no English players. There are only Lions. If you've 30 of them, one for everybody, you're welcome, we will take them. But there's no division."

His attitude to winning or losing was also critical, as he once explained. "It was this old thing of it's not the winning or the losing, it's the taking part that counts. That was a load of bullshit. You went out to South Africa to beat the Springboks in a series."

And beat them they did, winning three of the four Tests and drawing the other. As famous as the victory was his '99' call, which was deployed whenever a teammate was subjected to violent play and entailed Lions players clobbering their nearest opponent, the message being that the tourists wouldn't be intimidated. Legendary as the call is, McBride plays it down. "It has been overplayed. I would say there were possibly four incidents in all the games and that was about it. It was a good thing because it showed South Africa that the Lions at last were going to stand up and weren't going to take this nonsense. On previous tours they were bullied and we weren't prepared to accept it on this tour."

McBride retired the following year and made his last Ireland appearance in Cardiff, with his side crashing to a 32-4 defeat to Wales. All told he led his country on 12 occasions during his 63-cap career, as well as captaining a World XV against South Africa in 1977.

Legends of **RUGBY**

COLIN MEADS

When Rugby World, the world's best-selling rugby magazine, was launched in 1960, there was really only one choice as to who to put on the cover: Colin Meads. The man known throughout the rugby world as Pinetree was the archetypal New Zealand rugby player: tough, uncompromising and, above all, a man who had the game in his soul.

Meads, whose brother Stan was also an All Black, played almost all his international rugby at lock but also featured as a flanker and No 8. A cult figure throughout New Zealand, his home in the aptly named King Country is now a favourite tourist spot, with hundreds of Lions fans who travelled to New Zealand in 2005 taking the time to visit it during their trip.

Legend has it that as part of the training Meads did on his farm, he would run with a sheep under each arm. That adoration is magnified in New Zealand where there is a Colin Meads club, where members wear No 5 jerseys and meet to talk about the great man while reading from his autobiography, Colin Meads: All Black.

His toughness was perhaps best demonstrated in 1970, when he broke his arm playing in South Africa against Eastern Transvaal. Meads emerged from a ruck with a fearful injury but not only did he refuse to leave the field, in one of the hardest places to play rugby in the world, but he finished the match, reportedly saying afterwards: "At least we won the bloody game."

Dubbed 'Pinetree' by his team-mate Kevin Briscoe on the 1958 New Zealand Under-23s tour of Japan, it was an apt nickname and it stuck.

One of the first names on the All Blacks team sheet after his debut in 1957, Meads barely missed a match until his final Test, against the Lions in 1971. That series defeat by the Lions, when Meads was the All Blacks captain, proved a rare low point. His nadir had come in 1967, when he became only the second player to be sent off in a Test match, dismissed by KD Kelleher against Scotland.

Meads was initially played on the flank as the All Blacks possessed fearsome locks in Nev MacEwan and 'Tiny' Hill, but he soon found his way into his more accustomed No 5 shirt.

After representing King Country at primary school and junior level, Meads made his senior representative debut as a 19-year-old against South Auckland Counties in 1955, marking his debut not only with a try but incredibly with a drop-goal too. He was later to score seven Test tries.

His Test debut came in 1957 against Australia, but it was in 1960 when he became a legend on the world stage, going on tour to South Africa.

When England toured Australia in the summer of 2006, they played two Test matches, albeit in six days, and then returned to Blighty for an 11-week rest period before the new season. But when the All Blacks went to South Africa in 1960 they played 25 games, the teak-solid Meads featuring in 20 of them.

The All Blacks were imperious in the 1960s and Meads was at the core of their success. From 1965 to

Name: Colin Earl Meads
Born: 3 June 1936
Country: New Zealand
Position: Lock
Debut: 25 May 1957 v Australia
Caps: 55
Points: 2

Legends of **RUGBY**

COLIN MEADS

LEFT
A man of teak, Meads was one of the greatest All Blacks.

BELOW
Almost every honour the game had to offer arrived at Meads' door.

1969, they won a world-record 17 consecutive Tests, as the All Blacks forwards redefined the game.

In Meads's day, of course, there was no World Cup or Super 14 to trophy to hold aloft, so Meads gained his honours from his peers. Although he had his detractors, who claimed his physicality went too far – notably when he ended the career of Australia scrum-half Ken Catchpole in 1968 – he was named Player of the Century at the NZRFU Awards dinner in 1999.

There was no greater honour for Meads than to wear the All Blacks jersey, but in the rest of the world his abilities were recognised when he was invited to play in the South African 75th jubilee (1964), the RFU centenary matches (1971) and captained the President's XV and an Invitation XV against the All Blacks in 1973.

Meads wasn't content with holding an exalted place as a player and went on to be a leading coach and administrator, today still being one of the foremost commentators on New Zealand rugby.

A coach with King Country in the late 1970s, he soon progressed to becoming a national selector, a role he lost when he was part of the outlawed Cavaliers side that went to South Africa in 1986.

After coaching King Country from 1976-81, Meads was a North Island selector 1982-85 before being elected to the national selection panel in 1986. However, he was voted off the panel at the end of that year after being "severely reprimanded" by the NZRFU for coaching the unofficial Cavaliers side.

Chairman of the King Country RFU in 1987, Meads was forgiven for his part in the Cavaliers tour, and elected to the NZRFU council in 1992, later managing the All Blacks in 1994-95.

Stepping down in 1996, he remains closely in touch with the game, recently being part of a panel that reported to the NZRFU on aspects of modern forward play.

Outside of rugby, Meads, after initially agreeing to help out for a year, has been involved since his playing days with the Intellectually Handicapped Children's Society, including serving on the national council.

"Meads received just about every honour the game bestowed, including membership of the International Hall of Fame and the New Zealand Sporting Hall of Fame," wrote Lindsay Knight in a profile for the New Zealand Rugby Museum. "There was no dispute when at the end of 1999, New Zealand Rugby Monthly magazine proclaimed him the New Zealand Player of the Century. And in the New Year Honours list of 2001 he was made a New Zealand Companion of Merit, the equivalent of the by then scrapped knighthoods.

"As a sporting legend, Meads is New Zealand's equivalent of Australia's Sir Donald Bradman or the United States of America's Babe Ruth."

Legends of **RUGBY**

CLIFF MORGAN

So often in life a peak follows a trough, and the same certainly applies to Welsh rugby. Following a lean post-war period, Wales finally sprung into action once more and at the centre of it all was Cliff Morgan, a fly-half of exceptional ability who would play a key role in securing not only a Grand Slam but a famous win over the All Blacks.

A talented soccer player, Morgan could potentially have made his name in the round-ball sport – his father rejected the opportunity to play for Tottenham Hotspur – but going to a grammar school soon knocked that idea out of him.

Instead, he ended up signing for Cardiff straight from school at the age of 16. At 20 years of age, he made his debut for Wales against Ireland. Facing him for the Irish was their awesome fly-half Jack Kyle, a player Morgan had marvelled at when he was a teenager. "Two years before I had gone to Penarth with my father to watch Kyle play for the Barbarians," wrote Morgan in his autobiography. " 'Now there's a player you ought to be like', my father had said. He was so beautifully balanced, and had this gift of lulling the opposition into a false sense of security."

While Kyle did teach Morgan a trick or two on his daunting debut, the Welshman came through his baptism of fire with flying colours, helped by the protective care of Rex Willis at scrum-half and Bleddyn Williams and Jack Matthews in the centre. Wales held Ireland to a 3-3 draw.

A losing Test against the Springboks followed in the winter before Morgan had a chance to complete a full Five Nations campaign the next year. Having appeared in the opening three wins of the campaign against England at Twickenham (8-6), Scotland in Cardiff (11-0) and Ireland at Lansdowne Road (14-3), Morgan broke a fibula in a club game against Leicester and was ruled out for the season. It was hard on him, as he had to watch from the stands as Alun Thomas took his place and grabbed a drop-goal to help Wales secure the Grand Slam. "I went to watch and it's funny how selfish you feel in that situation," wrote Morgan. "I wanted Wales to win, yet I didn't want Alun to play too well at outside-half. Then he dropped a goal, which wasn't at all surprising; he was a class act was Alun Thomas."

Morgan returned to the fray for the second game of the Five Nations in 1953 and helped Wales to wins over Scotland, Ireland and France. But as they'd already lost to England, they finished runners-up.

That was more than made up for, however, with the unique double Morgan was part of against the All Blacks. Not only did his Cardiff side manage to turn over the mystical Kiwis 8-3, but he repeated the trick in the colours of Wales as the tourists were beaten 13-8. "I don't think we were a better team than New Zealand," penned Morgan, "but there was a certain spirit in the Welsh side that pulled us through. In those last ten minutes we defended, we fell, we tackled, we caught the

Name: Clifford Isaac Morgan
Born: 7 April 1930
Country: Wales
Position: Fly-half
Debut: 10 March 1951 v Ireland
Caps: 29
Points: 9

CLIFF MORGAN

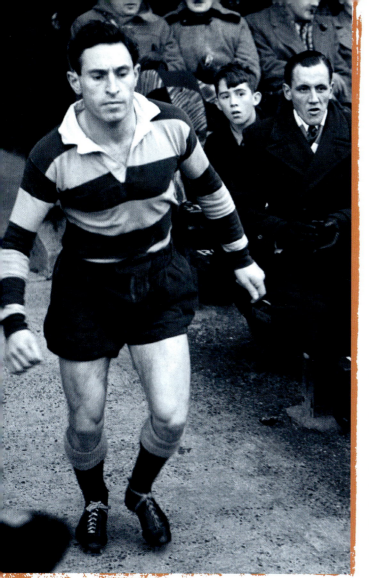

LEFT
Morgan made his name in the famous Cardiff shirt.

BELOW
A Lion in 1955, he became a legend in South Africa.

Thompson was injured ahead of the third Test in Pretoria, Morgan took over the captaincy, and he inspired his side to a 9-6 victory. "I was glad to have Clem [Thomas] around," said Morgan of that titanic clash. "I was a coward, really. I hated tackling and I didn't like falling on the ball in front of those man-eating South African forwards, but it had to be done in that match. Anyway, Clem looked after us."

The fourth Test may have been lost and the series drawn 2-2, but Cliff Morgan, the miner's son from Rhondda, had left an enormous impression on South African rugby.

Morgan captained Wales to the Five Nations crown the following year and helped them to another couple of top-two finishes before hanging up his boots in 1958. He had been lined up to captain the 1959 Lions tour to New Zealand but felt he could no longer afford to take the time off work.

His headline-grabbing days weren't over, however, as Morgan embarked on a successful career with the BBC, eventually becoming head of outside broadcasts despite suffering a stroke when he was 41. It was Morgan who provided the now immortal commentary to the most famous try of all time – the one scored by Gareth Edwards against the All Blacks in 1973.

ball, scooped it away to touch. All the little things that mattered."

After helping Wales finish joint top of the Five Nations with France in 1954, Morgan headed off on an adventure to Ireland, where he played for Dublin side Bective Rangers – who were promptly renamed Morgan Rangers! "There was lots of nonsense in the Irish papers about Welsh Magicians and Morgan Rangers and so on," said Morgan, who had moved to Ireland to manage a company manufacturing wire ropes. "But whatever I did for Bective was matched by what playing for them did for me."

Playing out of his home country didn't affect his international career as he was selected for the 1955 Lions tour to South Africa – a series that was to live long in the memory. A try in the Lions' 23-22 first-Test victory saw Morgan stamp his mark on the tour, and that was only the beginning. When regular Lions captain Robin

Even from behind the mike, Morgan was a legend: "Kirkpatrick to Williams. This is great stuff. Phil Bennett covering, chased by Alistair Scown. Brilliant, oh, that's brilliant. John Williams… Pullin, John Dawes. Great dummy. David, Tom David, the halfway line. Brilliant by Quinnell. This is Gareth Edwards. A dramatic start. What a score!"

Legends of **RUGBY**

GEORGE NEPIA

The 'Invincibles' were a side unlike any other the rugby world has seen. To be singled out as the finest rugby team to come from your country is one thing, but to do that when your country happens to be New Zealand is something different altogether. Even today, this team still enjoys global fame; rugby museums put on exhibitions based around them and kit manufacturers produce shirts based around their 1920s design. They were quite simply a phenomenon and the facts more than back it up.

From September 1924 until February 1925, the Invincibles played 32 games across Britain, Ireland, France and Canada. The itinerary included four Test matches against Ireland, England, Wales and France.

Throughout the whole tour, they remained unbeaten, winning all 32 contests, scoring 838 points and conceding just 116.

At the forefront of this feat, playing in every single match, was a young man called George Nepia, aged just 19. Like the Invincibles, his name has become immortal in rugby circles and he is still talked of as one of the greatest full-backs ever to grace a sports field.

A student of Wairoa and Nuhaka Native Schools and Maori Agricultural College (where he was taught by elders how to kick), he was unearthed by Hawke's Bay or, more specifically, their coach Norman McKenzie.

Nepia was a member of the province's Ranfurly Shield side of 1923, and in 1924 so impressive was Nepia at full-back in a North v South Maori encounter that the attentions of the national selectors were drawn to the teenager.

Two All Black trials later and Nepia – weighing in at 13st 1lb and 5ft 9in tall, a good size for the era – was on his way on the tour that would make him a Kiwi rugby legend. Fearsome with the boot and in the tackle, and wonderfully adept at fielding the ball, Nepia won the admiration of the British journalists covering the Invincibles' tour. One writer commented: "When I hear others debating who will play at full-back for the Kingdom of Heaven versus The Rest, I turn to stone. It is not for me to question whether Nepia was the best full-back in history. It is a question of which of the others is fit to loose the laces of his Cotton Oxford boots."

A further testament to his influence on that tour came when he was named as one of five Players of the Year by the English Wisden Rugby Almanack.

Over the course of the tour, Nepia scored 77 points for the All Blacks and he clearly deserved every bit of credit he was given. Famed New Zealand writer Terry

Name: George Nepia
Born: 25 April 1905
Country: New Zealand
Position: Full-back
Debut: 1 November 1924 v Ireland
Caps: 9
Points: 5

GEORGE NEPIA

LEFT
George Nepia relaxes, taking tea on his arrival in the UK.

BELOW
George Nepia kicking towards goal, 1924.

McLean penned Nepia's autobiography I George Nepia, and he said of one of the great man's performances: "Nepia had delivered to a pakeha's game (pakeha is the Maori word for 'white man') the outstanding qualities of Maori warriorhood – strength, pride, determination, craft and skill."

Sadly for New Zealand rugby, Nepia played only a handful more games for his country after such an astounding opening chapter to his international career.

He was stopped from touring South Africa, along with one other team-mate, because of race restrictions imposed by that country.

He did manage to turn out once more against New South Wales and then appeared in a Test against Australia in 1929, but he didn't finish the game following a back injury.

His last games for the All Blacks came during the visit of the British & Irish Lions in 1930. Following a warm-up match against North Otago, Nepia appeared in all four Tests against the tourists. He ended on a high note, too, with a 3-1 series win, though the fact he was still just 25 years of age shows what the rugby world missed.

Five years later, Nepia made the move to British rugby league. Despite being 30 by this time, he made a success of it, playing for London side Streatham & Mitcham before transferring to Halifax in Yorkshire during the 1936-37 season.

His impact on league was instant, particularly at Streatham & Mitcham, where his presence encouraged hundreds of youngsters to pick up the game. Crowds of up to 20,000 were attracted to watch him.

Returning to New Zealand in 1937, Nepia made a league international appearance for New Zealand in a 16-15 win over Australia and was then reinstated to rugby union after World War Two. Aged 42, Nepia amazingly turned out twice more for East Coast.

After eventually retiring, Nepia continued to be involved in the game as a referee throughout the 1950s.

Even with his early exit from the international scene, Nepia managed 129 first-class matches, including 46 for the All Blacks, 24 Maori games and 43 provincial appearances.

That the name George Nepia is still well known in rugby more than 70 years after his last Test cap shows how much of a talent the Wairoa-born full-back was. In 1986, a television channel in New Zealand broadcast a This Is Your Life show for Nepia. Almost 1.2 million Kiwis tuned in to give the show one of its highest ever ratings and, shortly after it aired, the 81-year-old Nepia passed away.

Legends of **RUGBY**

BRIAN O'DRISCOLL

The icon of modern-day Irish rugby, Brian O'Driscoll is the finest centre in the world. A student of Blackrock College and University College Dublin, he earned his representative spurs with Ireland Schools before being hurried through the ranks at Under-19 and Under-21 level ahead of his senior Test debut, against Australia on Ireland's 1999 summer tour.

Ireland may have been well beaten that day in Brisbane – 46-10 – but the significance of the occasion was worth more than any victory could bring. After some painfully lean years, Irish rugby finally had something to smile about, for in O'Driscoll they clearly had a world-class player in the making.

While initially the true depth of his talent was pretty much known only in Ireland, that was about to change in dramatic circumstances. In the 2000 Six Nations, O'Driscoll announced himself on the international scene in the most emphatic style with a stunning performance in Paris. Ireland snatched a thrilling 27-25 win against France thanks to three tries from O'Driscoll. It was Ireland's first win in Paris for 28 years, and took them to third in the championship, quite a turnaround considering they had finished bottom in three of the previous four years.

It was a taste of things to come, as Ireland's rejuvenation as a force in northern hemisphere rugby would coincide with the rise of this special talent from Leinster. The following year, the Dubliner's dancing feet again proved Ireland's inspiration as he helped them to second spot in the Six Nations and put France to the sword yet again, scoring his ninth international try in the 22-15 win.

With the Irish public already eating from the palm of his hand, the 22-year-old decided to show the rest of the world what he had to offer as well. His performances for Ireland made him an automatic choice for the Lions squad. And with Australia, home of the reigning world champions, the destination, it was going to be a step up for the young back. But whereas other players might have crumbled under the pressure of a Lions tour, O'Driscoll took it all in his stride and thrived in coach Graham Henry's side. The trip may have ended unsuccessfully for the tourists, but O'Driscoll mania was up and running. As he ran the Australian defences ragged, the tens of thousands of Lions supporters lifted the rafters of many a stadium with their renditions of Waltzing O'Driscoll, notably after he scored a fabulous try in the first Test at the Gabba.

Another Six Nations arrived and so did another O'Driscoll hat-trick, this time against Scotland in 2002. Even with defences paying him far closer attention thanks to his deeds Down Under, he was still an

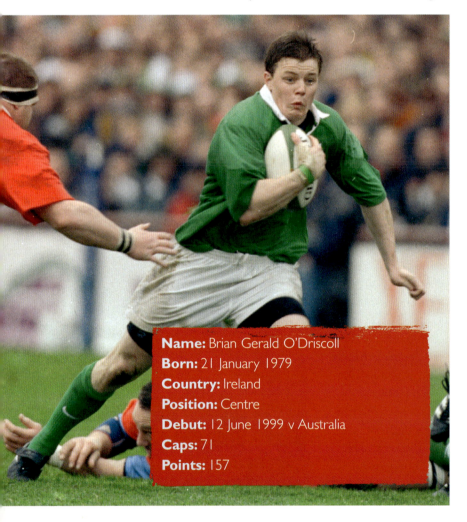

Name: Brian Gerald O'Driscoll
Born: 21 January 1979
Country: Ireland
Position: Centre
Debut: 12 June 1999 v Australia
Caps: 71
Points: 157

Legends of **RUGBY**

BRIAN O'DRISCOLL

LEFT
O'Driscoll playing for Ireland is tackled by Marco Bortolami of Italy during their Six Nations game, 2004.

BELOW
O'Driscoll in training for The Lions, 2005.

O'Driscoll's popularity in Ireland has elevated to him godlike status. He's been voted the country's sexiest man, been the inspiration for the printing of thousands of 'In God We Trust' T-shirts and has been a regular on both the front and back of newspapers. Think Gavin Henson-mania but swap one season for six and you're getting close to his status in Ireland.

While the 2005 Six Nations saw Ireland fall away in the last two games just as a potential Grand Slam beckoned, O'Driscoll still achieved even higher accolades when he was named captain of Clive Woodward's Lions tour to New Zealand. This time, however, the story didn't have a happy ending as he managed just one minute of the first Test before he was brought crashing to earth by an infamous 'spear' tackle, inflicted by Tana Umaga and Keven Mealamu.

The tackle dislocated his shoulder and delayed his start to the 2005-06 season. But he returned in time to boost Leinster's Heineken Cup charge, producing a magnificent display against Bath to help his province through to the quarter-finals. He followed up with a crucial try as Leinster claimed the scalp of reigning champions Toulouse in the last eight.

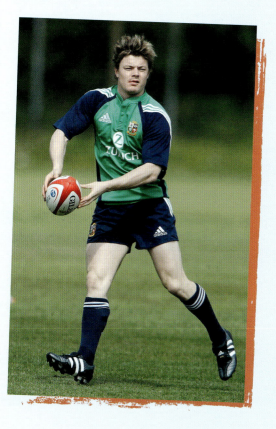

Following a poor autumn, Ireland had been written off by all and sundry for the Six Nations but a sensational purple patch in Paris was the turning point as Ireland racked up wins over Wales, Italy, Scotland and England. Two Triple Crowns in three years and O'Driscoll was at the centre of both of them. Before he came along, Ireland used to struggle; since his arrival, they've become a genuine force. It's no coincidence.

impossible man to tie down. The tries continued to flow and in Italy in 2003 he marked his 35th Ireland Test by scoring his 18th try, overtaking Brendan Mullin as Ireland's most prolific try-scorer.

Later, after wing Denis Hickie had challenged that mantle, O'Driscoll went to the top of the try charts again thanks to his efforts against France and England in the 2005 Six Nations. By the end of the 2006 tournament, he had bagged 27 tries in 64 Tests for Ireland.

Yet the tries tell only a fraction of the story. O'Driscoll performs all the basic skills better than almost anyone, as evidenced by the fact that he offloaded more times in the tackle than any other player in the 2006 Six Nations. His influence on Ireland is immense. He captained them for the first time against Australia in 2002 and with phenomenal effect as his troops dug out a famous 18-9 victory at Lansdowne Road.

With Keith Wood retiring after the 2003 World Cup, O'Driscoll was the obvious choice as successor and, like so many great players, the pressure that came with the job was water off a duck's back to him. He resumed his reign as captain in spectacular style, Ireland beating England at 'fortress' Twickenham to become the first side to defeat the newly crowned world champions. Having already beaten Wales in the opening fixture, another victory over Scotland secured second spot in the championship and, more importantly, Ireland's first Triple Crown since 1985.

Legends of **RUGBY**

FABIEN PELOUS

While New Zealand are likely to be favourites at the 2007 World Cup, France have a familiarity about them that's reminiscent of the current world champions when it comes to their on-field leader.

Just as England had a mighty, dark and brooding figurehead taking them into battle, so do France. A man of few words other than those used to give simple commands, someone who lets their play do the talking and a lock who has the ability to take a game, and his team, by the scruff of the neck and drag it up to the standards he expects. For Martin Johnson, read Fabien Pelous.

"He used to get a bit stressed about the captaincy but he has greater maturity and stature now and is happy to take the responsibility," said France team manager Jo Maso. "He is like Martin Johnson, whose character gave confidence to the whole England team. He gives us solidarity, he is our leader in battle and an example for the others to follow."

Even the English agree, as Brian Moore wrote in The Daily Telegraph. "It is Pelous who has to set the tone for the challenge mounted by the French. He leads in the heat of battle and from him is taken the soul of the side."

The 6ft 6in lock made his France debut in 1995 against Romania when he grabbed the first of his seven Test tries to date in a 52-8 rout. He's been a regular ever since, racking up 107 caps by the end of the 2006 Six Nations and becoming the most capped lock of all time. He captained France for the first time in 1997 in a 40-32 defeat to Italy and then for a run of 13 games in 2000 and 2001, a spell that saw France claim some impressive scalps, including a 42-33 win over New Zealand in Marseille.

Taking the armband on a handful of occasions in the next couple of years, he was eventually named long-term successor to Fabien Galthié as France captain following the 2003 World Cup in Australia. "Fabien Pelous has been an exemplary captain. It's good to have a man like him because we know we can build up the future of our team around him," said France coach Bernard Laporte of the man he has entrusted as his leader.

Former France captain Raphaël Ibanez, hooker for their 2006 Six Nations campaign, is another who's full of praise for Pelous – not least because of the manner in which he responded to a nine-week suspension for elbowing Australian hooker Brendan Cannon in the autumn of 2005.

"He's a natural leader, he doesn't need to say too much to us and we just follow him," said Ibanez. "He

Name: Fabien Pelous
Born: 7 December 1973
Country: France
Position: Lock
Debut: 17 October 1995 v Romania
Caps: 110
Points: 35

Legends of **RUGBY**

FABIEN PELOUS

LEFT
Pelous on the charge for France against Australia, 2004.

BELOW
French captain Fabien Pelous wins a line-out ball during a game against Italy in the Six Nations, 2005.

high. As part of the French side, Pelous had already had his fair share of success, including Grand Slams in 1997, 1998 and 2002. The 2004 one, though, was a bit special, not only because it was his first as captain but also because England, the world champions, were defeated 24-21 along the way. "They're all different," he said of the 2004 title, "but this seems the most satisfying because of the consistent way that we played. I have a very special feeling to be part of such a great squad.

"Nothing's changed. England are still the world champions; you can never take that away from them. We, though, have taken over the leadership in Europe."

Without ever really hitting top gear, France took the 2006 title as well, despite losing their opening game to Scotland. "At the beginning of the tournament we didn't think we would win the trophy but we worked a lot and now we can take the trophy to France," said Pelous. "For that I am very proud of my players."

As captain of Toulouse, Pelous has also led his club side to two Heineken Cup titles, another feat he shares with Johnson. Like his international colleagues, his team-mates at Toulouse have the utmost respect for Pelous. "He has been in the French squad for over ten years, and he brings great leadership qualities to the job, which is why Laporte has him there," said Irish forward Trevor Brennan. "He is the most capped French forward ever, and brings a bit of hardness to the team. He might not be the most flashy of players – he doesn't fling the ball around – but he is very fit for his age, works hard in training and in matches, and he has all the physical presence you could need."

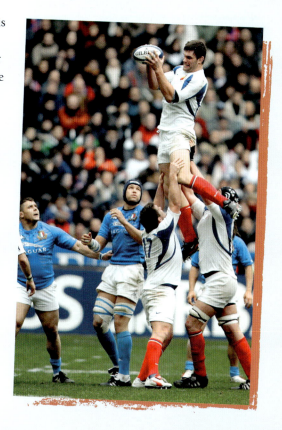

was suspended for a while and it took him a while to find his best form but he's done that now and he's so important to the team."

Disciplinary lapses are part and parcel of the aggressive game played by Pelous and, however rose-tinted English fans' glasses may be, few would ever suggest Johnson was whiter than white on the playing field.

During his time with France, Pelous has seen plenty of ups and downs, including two World Cups in 1999 and 2003. In the first he was part of a side that stunned the rugby world by dumping favourites New Zealand – complete with a rampant Jonah Lomu – out of the competition in the semi-finals by an eye-catching 43-31 scoreline.

Unhappily for les Bleus, they were unable to produce a follow-up and collapsed 35-12 to Australia in a disappointing final.

A similarly limp surrender came four years later. Without ever having truly got out of first gear, France found themselves again pitted against the tournament favourites – this time England. But whereas previously they found the fight in them, they couldn't repeat it in Sydney and fell to a lacklustre 24-7 loss.

Pelous, though, was to take some measure of revenge the following year, albeit with the stakes not quite so

Legends of **RUGBY**

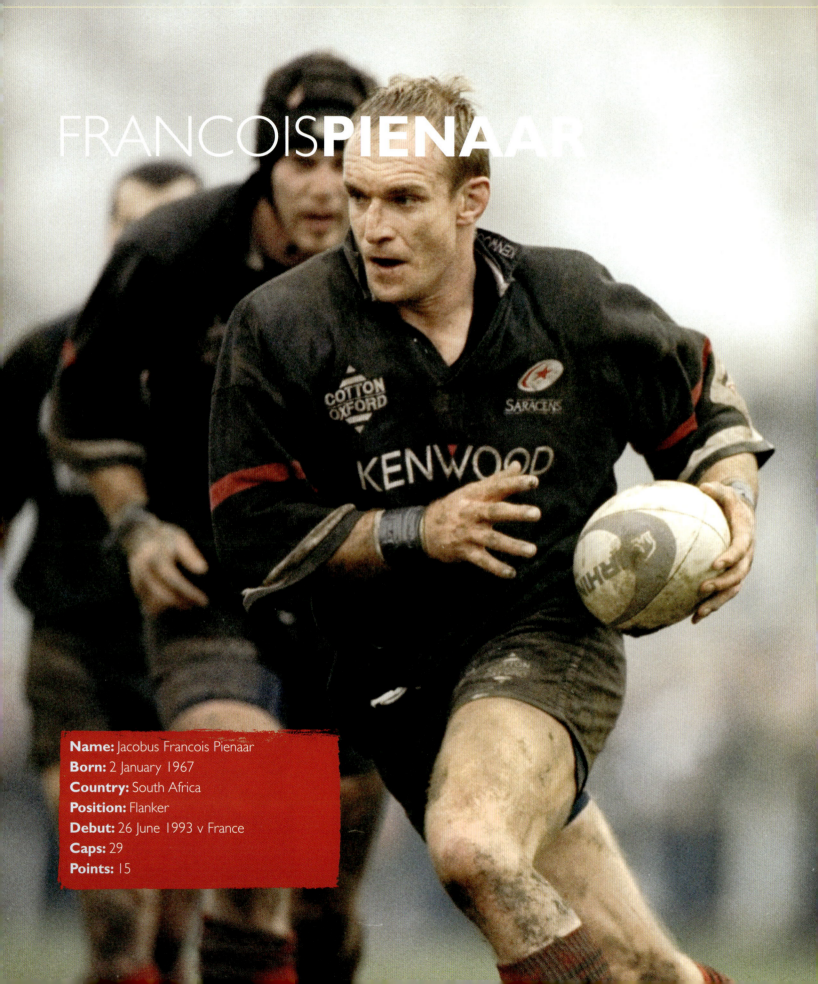

FRANCOIS PIENAAR

Name: Jacobus Francois Pienaar
Born: 2 January 1967
Country: South Africa
Position: Flanker
Debut: 26 June 1993 v France
Caps: 29
Points: 15

FRANCOIS PIENAAR

It could be argued that every World Cup final is special to those involved, and every image of a captain lifting that famous trophy is poignant in its way – whether it be David Kirk in 1987, Nick Farr-Jones in 1991, John Eales in 1999 or Martin Johnson in 2003. But there is one final that stands head and shoulders above the rest: the 1995 World Cup in South Africa. The moment Springboks skipper Francois Pienaar accepted the Webb Ellis Cup from South African president Nelson Mandela will live long in the memory of not only their countrymen but also everyone who was able to witness it, either in person or as one of the millions tuned into the final.

Sadly for such a great team, the fact that New Zealand were even there was insignificant.

Timing is, of course, everything and the story of how Pienaar's men won the World Cup for South Africa – at the first time of asking, after the country had been excluded from the events in 1987 and 1991 – symbolised the change taking place in the Rainbow Nation. That it was Pienaar, a blond, white Afrikaner, who collected the trophy from Mandela, the black leader who had brought about such fundamental change in South Africa, made the moment all the more unique. And the fact Mandela wore a replica of Pienaar's No 6 shirt summed up the new spirit of unity that prevailed in the Republic at that time. "It's been the best six weeks of my life," said Pienaar in the moments after the match. "We did not have 63,000 fans behind us today, we had 43 million South Africans.

Reflecting later on the momentous presentation at Ellis Park, Pienaar said: "When he gave us the trophy he said: 'Thank you for what you have done for South Africa'. I said we could never do what he had done for South Africa. I almost felt like hugging him but it wasn't appropriate, I guess."

As a player Pienaar, a hard-hitting blindside flanker, was clearly talented, but it was his leadership skills that stood him apart. From his very first cap against France in 1993, he was made captain (replacing the legendary Naas Botha) and he never relinquished the armband until the last of his 29 appearances in 1996, a 29-18 defeat against New Zealand.

His ability to lead was certainly put to the test. During the 1995 World Cup, South Africa's semi-final against France was in danger of being called off due to heavy rain. Had that decision been taken, France would have proceeded to the final because of South Africa's poor disciplinary record earlier in the competition. While the side waited to hear their fate, Pienaar's charisma and leadership came to the fore.

"Francois Pienaar, in the two hours before that World Cup semi-final, was brilliant," wrote Springbok wing Chester Williams in his autobiography. "He showed calmness, composure and enthusiasm. He kept focusing on the occasion and he kept channelling all the energy towards the match. At no stage did he look rattled. He communicated what was going on as if it were all part of the master plan.

"I don't believe Pienaar should have captained South Africa at the World Cup. I don't think he deserved to be there as a player… but I will never detract from Pienaar's

BELOW
Francois Pienaar checks the frozen ground after his debut match for the Saracens is called off in 1996.

Legends of **RUGBY**

FRANCOIS PIENAAR

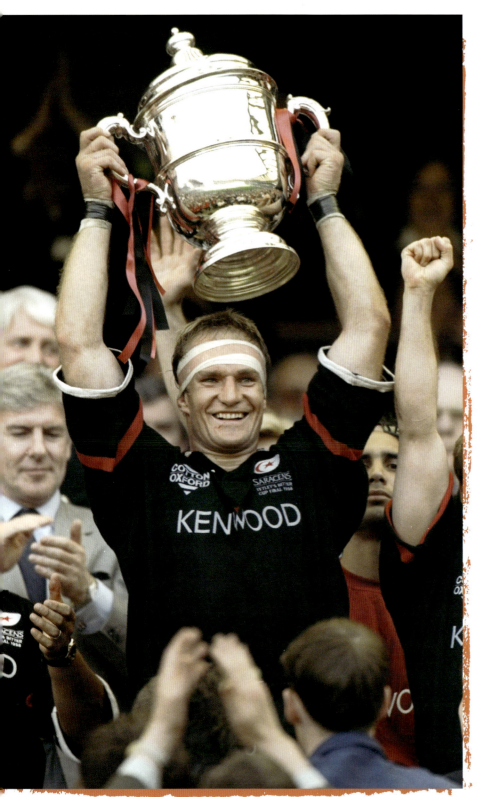

contribution to our victory in the changing room that Saturday. It was pivotal to our attitude when we eventually got on to the field. It was crucial to us being crowned world champions a week later when we beat the All Blacks in the final."

Hailing from a working-class Afrikaner family, Pienaar became a student of law at Rand Afrikaans University, gaining his place through an athletic scholarship. But on the field he didn't have the quickest rise to the top. He made his debut for the Springboks at the relatively late age of 26 having made his provincial debut for Transvaal (now the Golden Lions) four years previously.

In 1994, he captained Transvaal to Currie Cup success and such was his contribution to province and country that Rugby World awarded him the accolade of International Player of the Year.

His greatest moment came a year later with the World Cup triumph, something he recalls vividly. "I fell right to my knees," said Pienaar about the moment the cup was South Africa's. "I'm a Christian and I wanted to say a quick prayer for being in such a wonderful event, not because of the winning.

"Then all of a sudden I realised the whole team was around me, which was a special moment. Lifting the trophy was unbelievable. I can't describe the feeling as I wouldn't do it justice."

He wasn't to know it, but Pienaar's international career had little more than a year left to run. After eight more caps, which included a European tour and competing in the first-ever Tri-Nations, he was sensationally dropped by Andre Markgraaff in 1996. The coach accused him of feigning injury and a disgusted Pienaar never pulled on the green and gold jersey again.

Instead, he left South Africa for England to start a mini revolution at English club Saracens, initially as player-coach. With the floodgates having been

FAR LEFT
Pienaar brought silverware to Saracens, with their Tetley Bitter Cup final win, in 1998.

LEFT
Pienaar ended his career, in English rugby, with Saracens.

BELOW
Pienaar's greatest moment, receiving the World Cup trophy from President Nelson Mandela, in 1995.

opened due to the advent of professionalism, he was given an open chequebook to bring some of rugby's biggest names to the club. Unfortunately for him, Rob Andrew was given the same opportunity at Newcastle and subsequently beat him to the title. Saracens did, however, win the 1998 Tetley's Bitter Cup and qualified for the Heineken Cup. They've never looked like repeating Pienaar's early success since.

In 2000, Pienaar hung up his boots and added the role of chief executive to his coaching brief, but the failure to bring more silverware to the club cost him both jobs and he stepped down in 2002.

Legends of **RUGBY**

HUGO PORTA

For those who play outside the traditional 'big eight' rugby countries, gaining global recognition for your talents is no mean feat. You have to be something special.

Argentina's Hugo Porta was exactly that. A gifted footballer, Porta was almost lost to rugby when he was tempted to sign for Boca Juniors, but he eventually came to his senses and opted for the oval ball and club side Banco Nacion instead. It was a shrewd move, as he and the oval ball become solid friends. With the ball in hand, he could make the breaks, but using his boot he was simply awesome, whether controlling the game with tactical kicks, slotting penalties and conversions, or keeping the scoreboard ticking over with a smartly-taken drop-goal. All of it came easy to Porta, and Argentina had their first rugby superstar.

It was no accident that the ascent of Porta coincided with the rise of Argentine rugby. He made his debut against Chile in 1971 as the Pumas scraped past their South American counterparts 20-3 and 16 years later on his intended last cap (he was to return), he masterminded one of the greatest upsets in rugby history – a 27-19 win over Australia in Buenos Aires. Australia had the likes of Michael Lynagh and Nick Farr-Jones, Argentina had Porta, and it was Porta's 23 points that carried the day.

Such was life in Argentinean rugby that Porta would be playing against Paraguay one month, dishing out a 102-3 drubbing and landing 13 conversions, and the next New Zealand would be paying them a visit, Grant Fox, John Kirwan, David Kirk et al.

But opposition mattered little to Porta when it came to racking up the points. He registered 432 for Argentina in his astonishing 19-year international career.

From 1977 until his last match, Porta was an ever-present with the armband, save for three Tests against Paraguay, Chile and Uruguay. Captaincy seemed to bring out the best in him. In only his second Test as skipper, he kicked all of his side's points in an impressive 18-18 draw with France, the first of many occasions when the Goliaths of the rugby world were smote by his hand. In 1985 he stroked over 21 points to earn a draw with New Zealand, who less than two years later were to become the inaugural world champions. Results like this explain why even today Porta remains a legend of the game. The late Carwyn James was among his legion of fans. After the former Lions coach saw Porta play in 1980, he said: "It was a question of having one's faith restored in the aesthetic and artistic possibilities of back play."

Name: Hugo Porta
Born: 11 September 1951
Country: Argentina
Position: Fly-half
Debut: 10 October 1971 v Chile
Caps: 57
Points: 432

HUGO PORTA

The two wins over France in 1985 and 1986 further demonstrated Porta's worth to the national side. In the first, Porta notched up 16 points in the 24-16 win. The tally included a drop-goal, something of a Porta speciality as he would end his career with a remarkable 25 for the Pumas in Test rugby. In 1986, Argentina recorded a 15-13 win over the French, Porta responsible this time for 11 points.

The fly-half took Argentina to the first World Cup in 1987, although he couldn't stop his team going out at the pool stage as they fell to New Zealand (46-15, the closest any side in the group got to the All Blacks) and Fiji (28-9). However, a 25-16 win over Italy helped them finish level on points with every side in their pool apart from New Zealand.

Argentina's appearance on the world stage, coupled with that famous draw against the All Blacks two years previously, had helped raise the profile of rugby back home. It was a country on the up and nobody was going to underestimate the Pumas and get away with it.

The World Cup and the series against Australia that followed it were set to be Porta's parting shots, but he was persuaded to tour Britain three years later at the age of 39. It started brightly enough as Porta took 14 points to help run Ireland close in the opening game by a 20-18

scoreline, but it went rapidly downhill. England thumped the tourists 51-0 and Scotland did likewise, 49-3.

It wasn't only in the shirt of Argentina that Porta gained international recognition. Exiled from world sport, South Africa invited South America to tour and so the South America Jaguars came into being and paid them a few visits. Porta captained the side on three tours and in 1982 they even managed a win – by an astounding 21-12 margin in Bloemfontein. Needless to say, Porta grabbed all 21 points with a full house – try, conversion, drop-goal and four penalties. In total he scored 61 points for the invitational side during his eight appearances.

His experiences in South Africa helped Porta get the job of Argentinean ambassador in the country when he stopped playing. He held the post until he was appointed Minister for Sport in Argentina, a position he held from 1994 to 1999.

In April 1999, Porta turned out for Argentina against a World XV – and he still looked a class act at 47.

One story succinctly sums up what Porta meant to the people of Argentina; in 2000 his car was stolen by thieves in Buenos Aires, but once they'd discovered who it belonged to they returned it immediately.

It wasn't just because he played for one of the then second-tier rugby nations (Argentina are now rightfully at rugby's top table) that Porta stood out. In 1991, he was voted in Rugby World magazine as the best fly-half of all-time – proof that he would have been a special player no matter what nation he represented.

LEFT
Porta, aged 47 came out of retirement for a friendly match to celebrate the centenary of the Argentine rugby, in 1999.

BELOW
Porta in action against Ireland in 1990.

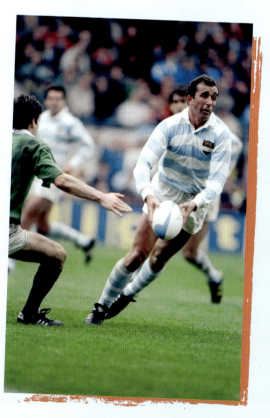

Legends of RUGBY

FRIK DU PREEZ

When Frik du Preez was declared South African rugby's Player of the 20th Century, there wasn't much dissent in one of the most passionate rugby countries in the world, such was his standing in the game. In many ways the award was remarkable as he survived challenges from modern-day players like Francois Pienaar and Joost van der Westhuizen, having played his final game for South Africa in 1971. It shows how untouchable he was.

Du Preez was an uncompromising second-row forward from Rustenberg, who ruled the roost in the unforgiving world of the pack for a decade.

He made his debut at Twickenham in 1961, immediately revealing his abilities to a European audience at a time when some of the greats from the southern hemisphere went unheralded in the north.

It comes as no surprise to discover that du Preez kicked off with a win in that clash against England (5-0) and from then until his final match in 1971, an 18-6 victory against Australia, he only suffered eight defeats in Springbok colours.

He made his debut as a second-row but also played on the flank in an international career that lasted 11 seasons. The abilities he picked up in the back row would serve him well throughout his career, and one of his most memorable moments came, as commentator Bill McLaren was often heard to say, "on the hoof".

That magic moment arrived in the 1968 series against the British & Irish Lions when, following a lineout, du Preez scored a storming try, running in from 40 metres with a lung-bursting, unstoppable dash. Tom Kiernan stood in front of him but, as the South African writer AC Parker vividly concluded, the Lions full-back might as well have tried to stop a locomotive going at full speed.

That try was typical of the all-round footballing skills demonstrated by du Preez. Of the more modern era, think John Eales and you are getting close to what du Preez was like. Both men were accomplished locks but also had skills rarely associated with those in the engine room. Each had superb handling ability, could get around the pitch swiftly and, most unusually, could kick goals, du Preez landing two penalties and a conversion in his Test-match career.

Those 1968 Springboks, with du Preez at their heart, inflicted a 3-0 series win on the Lions and a 2-0 victory in France. A year later, Australia were put to the sword in a 4-0 whitewash.

Name: Frederick Christoffel Hendrik du Preez
Born: 28 November 1935
Country: South Africa
Position: Lock
Debut: 7 January 1961 v England
Caps: 38
Points: 11

Legends of **RUGBY**

FRIK DU PREEZ

LEFT
Frik Du Preez tackles an opponent in a match against Southern Counties in 1960.

BELOW
Du Preez (top right) beats France's Elie Cester (top, left) to the line out ball during a Rest of the World training session, 1971.

Those who saw him in his pomp believe that du Preez, renowned as a man of great humility, would have suited modern-day rugby and would have thrived in a sport where ball-handling skills have become more paramount as the decades have passed.

He prospered in an era when lifting in the lineout wasn't allowed and his ability to leap from a standing start was legendary. Springbok team-mate Tiny Naude said: "Frik wasn't a very big man but he was very athletic. He could jump up to a man's waist, whereas when I jumped my feet hardly left the ground!"

The great Colin Meads remembers du Preez as an opponent who "could jump up and clap his hands above the crossbar," adding: "I struggled to touch the bloody thing."

Commentator McLaren was another one to recognise du Preez's pre-eminence in the lineout. "He was one of the greatest lineout technicians, with a standing jump measurement that was mind-boggling considering that he was only 6ft 2in and 15 and a half stone," said McLaren.

"Du Preez developed from a fly-half at school to become one of the most gifted locks of all time. He was a dependable lineout purveyor, with educated hands and a powerful boot, and a grinding scrummager who was astonishingly quick for his size. In his first ten Internationals he never lost. He once sent over a 75-yard dropped goal in Pretoria and he had the honour of leading the Springboks onto the field for his final Test, against Australia in 1971."

This man of many talents was rewarded for his endeavours when he was named as a founder member of the International Rugby Hall of Fame in 1997, only one of two Springboks (with Danie Craven) in that list of initial inductees.

Craven, for many years the man in charge of South African rugby, paid this tribute to du Preez: "South African rugby is an inspiration for everyone in our country who is interested in the game, and a source of wonder for those people beyond our borders. One of the most important factors responsible for this is the fact that throughout the history of Springbok rugby there have been great players and great personalities.

"Amongst these greats is Frik du Preez. As long as rugby is played in our country, people who know Frik or knew him, or people who heard of him or read about him, will have a connection with him, and that will enrich our rugby just as Frik did on the playing fields."

Du Preez's influence on the Springboks continued into the professional era, and along with Francois Pienaar he was chosen to hand out the shirts to the South Africa team during the 2005 Tri-Nations Championship.

When du Preez, who also played for Northern Transvaal, retired in 1971, he had won a record 38 caps for South Africa. Including his non-Test appearances, he played 87 times for South Africa, scoring an even 87 points.

Legends of **RUGBY**

JEAN-PIERRE **RIVES**

A recent recipient of the IRB's Spirit of Rugby award, Jean-Pierre Rives was the ultimate flanker of his generation, known for his uncompromising tackling, perfect handling skills and ability to appear all over the field and at all times – as if there were 15 identical blond-haired rugby machines on the pitch at once.

Born in Toulouse on New Year's Eve 1952, Rives began his rugby career with his local team. He appeared on the scene for France as a 22-year-old in 1975, the second season on the trot in which les Bleus had finished in the bottom two of the Five Nations table. Turning out against England, Scotland and Ireland, Rives enjoyed a 27-20 victory against their arch-rivals from across the Channel. Scotland were also beaten 10-9 in Paris, but Ireland – with Willie John McBride in their ranks – defeated them 25-6 at Lansdowne Road.

The following year, Scotland, Ireland and England were well beaten by the French, but it was the famous Welsh side that stopped Rives getting his hands on the title with a 19-13 win in Cardiff.

By this point, Rives was part of a deadly back-row trio also comprising Jean-Claude Skrela and Jean-Pierre Bastiat. As a unit, they would play a huge role in bringing success to French rugby during the 1970s.

The first part of that success followed in 1977 as they broke Wales' domination of the Five Nations with a Grand Slam that took a Herculean effort to achieve given the astounding strength of the side from the Principality.

The opening game of the campaign saw France take on the reigning champions in Paris and revenge was gained with a 16-9 win. The bandwagon was up and running and nobody was going to stop them. England ran them close, however, being beaten by the tightest of margins at Twickenham. Just one point separated the sides in a 4-3 away victory, centre Françcois Sangalli scoring the only try.

With the two toughest contenders out of the way, France eased past both Scotland and Ireland with 23-3 and 15-6 winning margins. France had won only their second Grand Slam ever, nine years after their first.

It was very nearly two Grand Slams on the trot the following season. Once again England, Scotland and Ireland were dealt with but the Welsh proved spoilsports yet again, beating France 16-7 courtesy of two tries from fly-half Phil Bennett.

Rives was named France captain in 1978 with his first game coming against Romania. The Oaks gave Rives's side a scare as the match ended 9-6 in France's favour.

He would captain them on 34 occasions by his retirement in 1984, at the time a world record for an international skipper.

Name: Jean-Pierre Rives
Born: 31 December 1952
Country: France
Position: Flanker
Debut: 1 February 1975 v England
Caps: 59
Points: 20

Legends of **RUGBY**

JEAN-PIERRE RIVES

LEFT
Rives plough's through the English defence during a Five Nations game in 1980.

BELOW
Jean-Pierre Rives pictured in 2002.

The first Five Nations under his leadership saw France again play second fiddle to Wales, but they did enough to secure the runners-up spot.

His greatest achievement as captain was just around the corner when France travelled to New Zealand for two Tests in 1979. In the first match the All Blacks ran out 23-9 victors, but in the second Test at Eden Park, France shocked the rugby world with their first win on New Zealand soil, by 24-9. It wasn't just the result that mattered, it was the style and swagger with which victory was gained. The French ran the All Blacks ragged with a brand of rugby that was to win them admirers the world over. They scored four tries that day and Rives was an inspiration to his team-mates.

Back on the European front and the Five Nations was going through a shake-up as the era of Welsh domination was coming to a close. The battle for supremacy was between England and France. England's captain Bill Beaumont knew what they had to do if they wanted to win their first Grand Slam since 1957.

"Our main tactic was to stop Jean-Pierre Rives," he said. "He was their truly outstanding player, both defensively and in attack. Mainly we just tried to keep him at the bottom of every ruck – it was the safest place for him. Unfortunately, this tactic didn't get off to a great start. Rives scored a try under the sticks after about two minutes and we were three down instantly."

On this occasion, Beaumont's side managed to claw their way back and France were beaten 17-13 in Paris by England for the first time in 16 years.

Rives didn't have long to wait for his first Grand Slam as captain, however. The following year, France stormed to the title unbeaten, their four wins including a 16-12 defeat of England on their own turf, repaying the favour from the year before.

It was Rives's last Grand Slam, although he did manage a share of the title with Ireland in 1983 when both sides gained three wins from four.

He retired a year later after the defeat by Scotland at Murrayfield, his final international match. Years of bashing opponents had taken its toll on his shoulder and recurring injuries forced his departure from the game he'd given so much to. He finished his career in Paris with Racing Club.

Outside of his feats with France, Rives toured South Wales twice with the Barbarians and turned out for them in prestigious fixtures with the British & Irish Lions and New Zealand.

After hanging up his boots, he turned his attentions to the world of art. As a sculptor in Paris, he was often seen mixing with the city's avant-garde. He has acted in several films, most notably in the 2000 movie The Druids alongside Christopher Lambert, and he owns a trendy restaurant in the French capital.

He has remained active in rugby circles and used his status as vice-president of France's Rugby Federation to help his country win the bid to stage the 2007 World Cup.

Legends of **RUGBY**

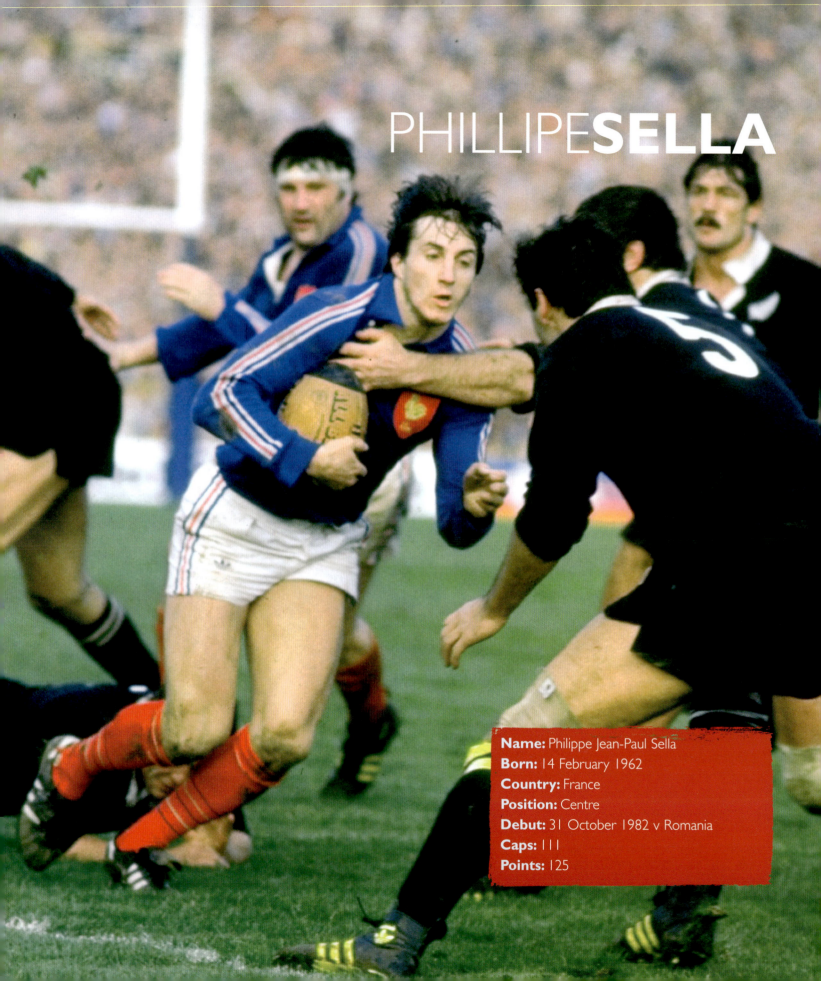

PHILLIPE SELLA

Name: Philippe Jean-Paul Sella
Born: 14 February 1962
Country: France
Position: Centre
Debut: 31 October 1982 v Romania
Caps: 111
Points: 125

PHILLIPE SELLA

One of the key exponents of France's champagne rugby, Philippe Sella's skill and magic is surpassed only by his incredible longevity. The centre stayed at the top of rugby's tree for 111 caps over 13 years, dazzling spectators and befuddling opponents. Sella wasn't shy of the rough stuff either, as former France coach Jacques Fouroux explained when he described him as having "the strength of a bull but the touch of a piano player". Following the 2006 Six Nations, Sella lay third in the all-time list for most capped players, four ahead of current France captain Fabien Pelous.

Jonathan Davies, in selecting Sella in his all-time Five Nations XV, was full of praise for the Frenchman. "Inside-centre is a spot where there is no competition. Philippe Sella was big, strong and quick. He scored tries and was defensively very sound. He played in a very good French side and one of the main reasons for that was because they had 'the Prince' at inside-centre."

Even though his international career started on the low that was defeat to Romania in 1982, Sella still stood out as a talent to watch, despite ending up in hospital for the night with concussion. An Agen player throughout his career until Saracens came calling, his ability to be both brutal and beautiful was admired by many, not least Jamie Salmon, who played in the centre for both New Zealand and England. "As an All Black I'd played against the excellent Roland Bertranne, but Sella was one of the first players to have a major physical presence in midfield."

Following the disappointment of defeat to Romania, Sella helped France to two victories over Argentina, scoring the first two of his 30 Test tries for France.

He was back on the scoresheet on his Five Nations debut at Twickenham, Les Bleus beating England 19-15 on their way to a tied championship with Ireland.

In the 1984 championship, Sella helped France win in Cardiff for the first time since 1968. While adding the scalps of Ireland and England, Scotland proved an insurmountable stumbling block and toppled the French 21-12 at Murrayfield. The win gave Scotland the Grand Slam and left France licking their wounds in second place.

A similar fate would befall them in 1985. This time France remained unbeaten, but draws with Ireland and England left them trailing the Irish in top spot.

The following year saw Sella take his game to new heights. He became one of the select few to score in every Five Nations match of a championship, with several memorable tries helping France to a shared title with the Scots. Against Ireland the ball went through 21 pairs of hands before Sella crossed the whitewash, against Wales he hauled several defenders with him as he touched down and against the English another flowing French move from their own half was brought to a successful conclusion by the Prince. The latter try prompted Nigel Starmer-Smith to proclaim that there was "no better tribute for the outstanding player in the championship".

The summer that followed included a drawn series with Argentina, and defeats by Australia and New Zealand. Later that year France took revenge against the All Blacks as the Kiwis fell 16-3 in Nantes. Admittedly, the New Zealanders had won the first Test 19-7 (with

BELOW
Philippe Sella on his way to scoring a try for France during their World Cup match against Fiji in 1991.

Legends of **RUGBY**

PHILLIPE SELLA

Sella scoring), but it was a huge win for the French nonetheless, with the inaugural World Cup looming at the end of the season.

Sella's brilliance of 1986 proved a foundation stone for unqualified success in the 1987 Five Nations as France claimed their first outright title since 1981 – and once again it was with a Grand Slam. The 19-15 away win over England featured one of Sella's finest moments, an interception score from deep inside his own half. "We were under big pressure from the English at the time and the game was still not won," recalled Sella. "I can't explain why exactly – maybe it's the French flair – but I intercepted the ball and 70 metres later had scored a try."

France were among the favourites for the World Cup that summer and they proved their standing with an epic 30-24 semi-final win over Australia in Sydney. Unfortunately, the European champions had little left to give and they were humbled 29-9 by New Zealand in a one-sided final.

Coping with World Cup disappointment in the only way they knew how, Sella's France took a share in the next Five Nations with Wales before winning the title outright in 1989. It was Sella's penultimate Five Nations title as they achieved it only once more – in 1993 – during his career.

The 1987 World Cup final was also to be Sella's grandest stage as England put paid to French hopes in the 1991 quarter-finals and the weather combined with an inspired South Africa to end their interest at the semi-final stage in 1995.

Sella bowed out of international rugby in the third-place play-off victory over England, before enjoying a successful spell at Saracens in his twilight years, the highlight being a sparkling cup final rout of Wasps in 1998. Sella played his last competitive game at 36.

Legends of **RUGBY**

FAR LEFT
Sella ended his career with 111 caps, a world record.

LEFT
A giant in the world game, here Sella leaves Scott Hastings in his wake.

BELOW
Sella with the ball, scores a try for France in the Five Nations against Wales.

Asked which of his caps he remembers most, Sella points to his 94th cap, against Australia at the Parc des Princes in 1993. "That was the day I broke Serge Blanco's record for international caps. Serge had rung me that morning to tell me he couldn't make it to the ceremony. When it came to distributing the jerseys, Pierre Berbizier, the coach, gave one to everyone except me. Then the changing-room door opened and in came Serge with my jersey in his hand. I have to admit I was fighting back the tears. That was one of the proudest moments of my career."

Legends of **RUGBY**

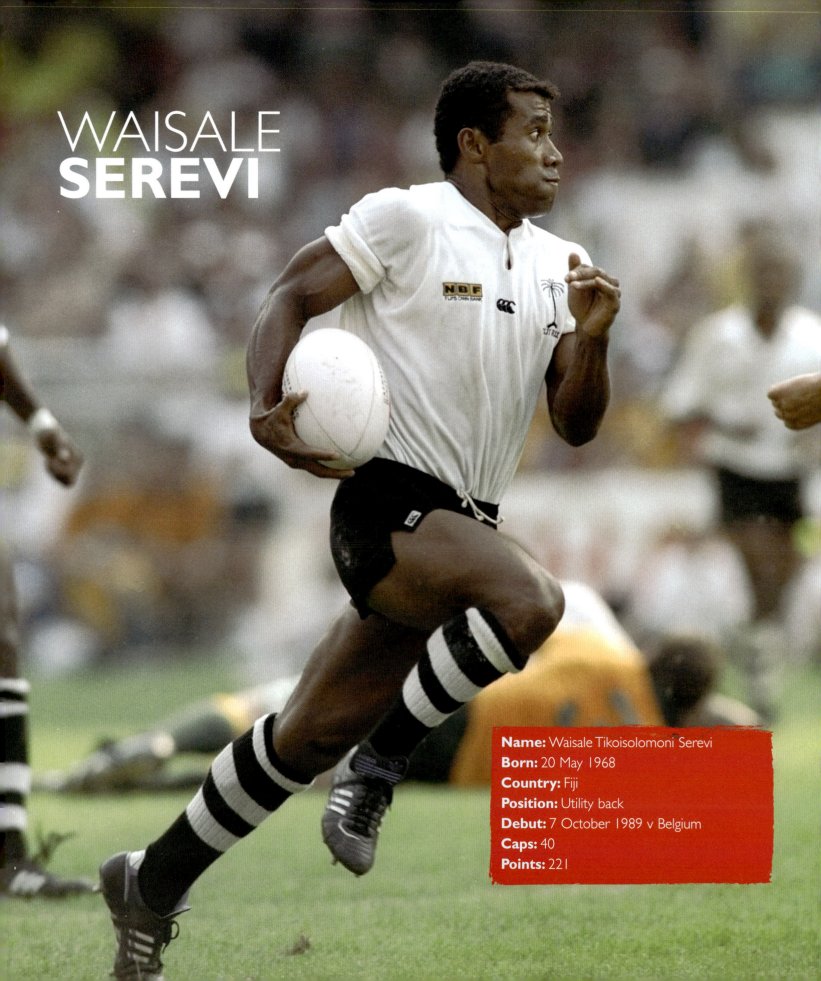

WAISALE
SEREVI

Name: Waisale Tikoisolomoni Serevi
Born: 20 May 1968
Country: Fiji
Position: Utility back
Debut: 7 October 1989 v Belgium
Caps: 40
Points: 221

WAISALE SEREVI

It's ironic that one of the greatest talents world rugby has seen never really made his mark in the 15-a-side game. Rarely has there been a player who can produce so much magic with the oval ball as Waisale Tikoisolomoni Serevi. With the skills to make the ball do things that mere mortals can only dream of doing, Suva-born Serevi has delighted fans the world over with his dazzling array of tricks, flicks and kicks. His vision is unparalleled; one minute he appears to be going nowhere but into a dead end, the next he's conjured some space and sent a team-mate scuttling in for another Serevi-inspired score.

But impressive as his skill set is, it's in the vast expanse of the sevens game that we have got to appreciate it most. While his sevens career has involved more gongs than a trophy-maker's workshop, his 15-a-side résumé is less striking.

It began in 1989 in Liege when Fiji took on the rugby minnow that is Belgium and ran amok, racking up 76 points with none in return. Serevi grabbed two scores in the far-from-glamorous fixture.

From such low-key beginnings, Serevi managed to win 40 caps for his country up until his international retirement at the 2003 World Cup. Scoring 221 Test points, he certainly made a contribution, especially when you consider that of the 40 caps, 16 were from the bench. And he achieved the feat of appearing at three World Cups, so even though his exploits in Test rugby aren't regarded as much to write home about, he still achieved far more than most.

On a club level, things were similarly stop-start. His talent was recognised by Australia's World Cup-winning coach Bob Dwyer, who snapped him for English club Leicester Tigers. But the presence of South African duo Joel Stransky at fly-half and Michael Horak at full-back forced Serevi onto the wing. Here, he was able to produce moments of brilliance, but his defensive frailties were also exposed as he managed to delight and disappoint the Welford Road faithful in equal measure. Failing to settle into the English game, he moved on to France and lower-level rugby at Stade Bordelais.

To talk about the negatives, however, is to downplay the contri-bution Serevi has made to the global game. He may have struggled with the 15-a-side format but in sevens he came alive. So much so that Serevi and the abridged game are synonymous with one another. Ask any rugby fan to name a sevens player and the answer will probably be Serevi, surely the greatest exponent of the sport there has been. And there are plenty of people to back that assertion up. Paul Treu, the South Africa sevens coach, said of the Fijian: "I played against Serevi and he was the master of the game; if people talked about sevens, they talked about Serevi."

Serevi's list of honours in the game speaks volumes: two World Cups (both as captain), five Hong Kong Sevens titles, two Commonwealth Games silver medals and a gold from the World Games is just the tip of the iceberg.

As if to consolidate his legendary status, Serevi completed a fairy-tale comeback at the 2005 Sevens World Cup in Hong Kong. In international exile and playing club rugby in the lower reaches of the English

BELOW
Serevi, a master of the Sevens game, evades a tackle.

WAISALE SEREVI

league with Staines, Fiji coach Wayne Pivac recalled the maestro for the World Cup. "He's a wee man who we call 'Wai'," said Pivac at the time. "He's world famous when it comes to sevens, he's a great guy, a good leader and obviously has been a fantastic player. He hasn't quite got the legs he had when he was 26. He's 36 now, but still he's got the vision and the class and knows the game inside out. He was one of the first people I wanted to get involved."

Pivac's decision to recall Serevi paid dividends as Fiji bucked the sevens trend that has seen the New Zealanders dominate the game in recent years. Not only did Fiji win but it was with a style and panache orchestrated by the master himself. In the semi-final, Serevi scored in sudden-death extra time to beat England 24-19. He then pulled the strings as Fiji toppled the Kiwis 29-19 in the final, reminding the world just why Serevi is so adored in his homeland. He was named Player of the Tournament and the feat of becoming world champions ensured that a public holiday was declared in Fiji.

Though his 38th birthday was to come and go before the end of the 2006 IRB Sevens series, Serevi was still going strong as player-coach of the Fiji side. And after their triumph in the Singapore Sevens in April, Fiji led the series by 10 points with just two events to go. New Zealand, perennial champions, were out of contention.

What, then, is the secret to Serevi's success? "I enjoy playing rugby, this is my

Legends of **RUGBY**

FAR LEFT
Serevi also won 40 caps for his country at 15-a-side.

LEFT
Here on his way to helping Fiji lift the World Sevens crown in 2005.

BELOW
Serevi in action for Fiji is tackled by two Kenyan players during their match at the Hong Kong Rugby Sevens tournament in 2006.

life," he said. "I look after myself, I don't drink and I don't smoke, so that's why I'm still enjoying playing rugby.

"They asked me when would I stop playing rugby, but while you still enjoy it day to day you might as well keep on doing it.

"One day I will stop. I didn't want to regret stopping this year and saying that I could have done one more year. I thank God for giving me the power and strength to keep playing and enjoying what I love best: playing rugby sevens."

The Fijians thank God for Serevi too.

Legends of **RUGBY**

FERGUS SLATTERY

Name: John Fergus Slattery
Born: 12 February 1949
Country: Ireland
Position: Flanker
Debut: 10 January 1970 v South Africa
Caps: 61
Points: 12

FERGUS SLATTERY

A 61-cap international, Fergus Slattery was a pivotal figure on the successful 1974 British & Irish Lions tour to South Africa, and part of the Ireland side that won the 1974 and 1982 Five Nations crowns and shared the title with France in 1983. He was also a forerunner to the modern-day flanker that we see today whose principal job is to scare the living daylights out of the fly-half.

Bill McLaren named Slattery in his all-time World XV and said of him in his book Dream Lions: "In that lengthy career he never departed from an all-action, dynamic style that marked him out as special. His pace about the paddock and to the breakdown, his ferocious tackling and his fitness, hardness and ball-winning capability made him highly respected and feared. Sundry stand-off halves have had their confidence and rhythm ruined by that hunting dog-type hounding of a Slattery who saw it as a main part of his function to disrupt opposing moves by placing instant pressure upon their ball-carrier, be he back or forward."

A student of Blackrock College and University College Dublin, Slattery was an estate agent by trade and was first capped by Ireland at the age of 20 in an 8-8 draw with South Africa in Dublin. Slattery was given credit for playing a vital part in keeping the Springboks at bay for much of the game. His non-stop harassing of the opposition would later prompt McLaren to comment: "With Fergus Slattery you just wound him up and sent him running – he just never stopped."

The flanker was then selected for the 1971 Lions tour to New Zealand – despite being just 22 – and was picked for the third Test, only for tonsillitis to end up costing him his first Lions cap. His time on rugby's greatest stage was still to come.

Three seasons of building an even bigger name for himself in the Five Nations followed before he tasted glory with Ireland for the first time in 1974. Two wins and a draw from the four games were enough to see the Irish top the table for the first time in 23 years.

Slattery had done enough in Ireland's Championship-winning side to earn a place on the 1974 tour to South Africa, although most assumed he would be fulfilling the role of understudy. As Clem Thomas wrote in his book The History of the British & Irish Lions: "Fergus Slattery was thought to be in the shadow of Tony Neary, but he showed such a tireless work rate and range of skills, most notably his knack of taking a tackle and riding over it before passing the ball to the support, that he easily held his Test place, and he was to retire as the world's most-capped flanker."

Never a regular try-scorer (he managed just three during his Ireland career), he was controversially denied a last-gasp score in the fourth Test at Ellis Park. Had it been awarded, the Lions would have gained an amazing whitewash over the Springboks. But today he plays it down, as he said in Lions Of Ireland: "Roger Uttley didn't touch down his try in the first half and in both that case and mine, Max Baise (the South African referee) was very badly positioned, he couldn't see what was going on. He made a call but was just in the wrong place. At the end of the day the result was probably fair because we didn't play well. I think you could sense it in the build-up; guys were packing their bags and preparing

BELOW
Irish flanker Fergus Slattery of The Lions at Astbourne, training ground, 1971.

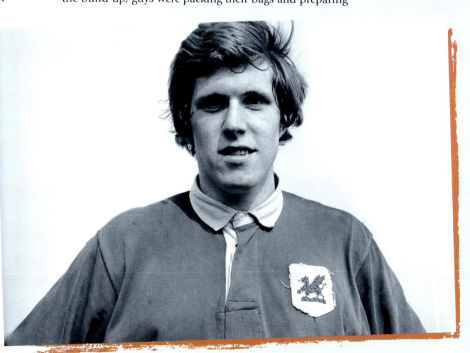

FERGUS SLATTERY

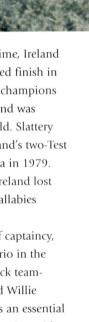

to go home, one or two guys played with injuries and we had lost a little focus… I don't think you can really say Baise cost us the win, but in general on Lions tours, local referees were a big factor."

Unfortunately for Slattery and the Lions, he was unavailable for selection in 1977, and so the 1974 tour was the last time the world would see him in the red shirt.

Back with Ireland and Slattery took over the captaincy of his country in 1979 for what was to be the beginning of a run of 17 consecutive matches at the helm. During that time, Ireland managed one second-placed finish in 1980 behind Grand Slam champions England before the armband was handed to Ciaran Fitzgerald. Slattery did, however, oversee Ireland's two-Test series victory over Australia in 1979. On an eight-match tour, Ireland lost only once and beat the Wallabies twice, 27-12 and 9-3.

Without the burden of captaincy, Slattery formed a deadly trio in the back row with his Blackrock teammates John O'Driscoll and Willie Duggan, and that unit was an essential element of Ireland's Five Nations title

FAR LEFT
Slattery pictured during the British Lions tour to South Africa in 1974.

LEFT
Slattery in action for The Lions during their Tour of New Zealand in 1971.

BELOW LEFT
Fergus Slattery has a joke as he borrows Willie John McBrides pipe, 1974.

win in 1982 and the shared crown in 1983. In total, they played 20 Internationals together for Ireland.

Slattery's final Test for Ireland came the following year in the 25-12 defeat by France in Paris.

He also turned out for the Barbarians on three occasions without defeat as part of the sides that beat the All Blacks (23-11, 1973) and Wallabies in Cardiff (19-7, 1976). His third game for the invitational side was a 13-13 draw with the New Zealanders at Twickenham in 1974.

Legends of **RUGBY**

GREGOR TOWNSEND

If anyone has made the most of the advantages that come with life as a professional rugby player, then it's Gregor Townsend. Not for him the monotony of being a one-club man; Townsend has plied his trade in Scotland, England, France and, uniquely for a professional British rugby player, in South Africa.

When you write about Townsend, use of the adjective 'mercurial' is virtually a legal requirement and, much as the man himself no doubts tires of hearing it, it has to be said it's fitting. Like Carlos Spencer of New Zealand, Townsend is capable of the kind of flicks and tricks that make paying to watch rugby a pleasure for the supporter.

Unfortunately, such brilliance comes at a cost. Trying to make something happen when nothing seems possible involves a high degree of risk and that means that good as it is when it comes off, sometimes it goes wrong. But even if it doesn't work on three occasions, when it does happen on the fourth then it's usually worth the wait.

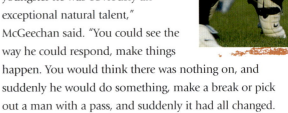

Capped 82 times for Scotland, mostly at fly-half but often too at centre, Townsend began his career at Gala, where he was spotted by Ian McGeechan as a precocious 18-year-old stand-off. " Even as a youngster he was obviously an exceptional natural talent," McGeechan said. "You could see the way he could respond, make things happen. You would think there was nothing on, and suddenly he would do something, make a break or pick out a man with a pass, and suddenly it had all changed. He had that rare ability to change the way the game went."

Townsend was later to link up with McGeechan at Northampton Saints in 1995. France was his next destination with Brive and then Castres before returning to Scotland and the Borders. Staying with the Scottish region up until the 2003 World Cup, Townsend's feet started itching again and he took up an offer from South African Super 12 side the Sharks to ply his trade in Natal for a season. A second visit to France and Montpellier was the next stop before eventually coming home to the Borders for the 2005-06 season.

During his globe-trotting adventures, Townsend has become one of the greats. The Scotsman named him as one of the top 20 Scottish players of all time and singled out his part in a famous 1995 match-winning try in Paris: "Townsend will perhaps be best remembered for that sublime reverse pass – taking two French defenders out the game – which sent Gavin Hastings through to score under the posts, and gave Scotland their first victory in Paris for nearly 30 years.

"At his best that's the sort of player Townsend is: a risk-taker, mesmerising and visionary in attack, and worth the admission money alone. At his worst, he can

Name: Gregor Peter John Townsend
Born: 26 April 1973
Country: Scotland
Position: Fly-half/Centre
Debut: 6 March 1993 v England
Caps: 82
Points: 164

GREGOR TOWNSEND

LEFT
Gregor Townsend of Scotland is tackled during the Rugby World in a game against Fiji, 2003.

BELOW
Townsend in action for Montpellier, 2005.

be frustratingly careless, too risky, too quick for his team-mates, and enough to make you tear your hair out. But by common consent he is one of the few Scottish players of recent years to be genuinely world-class.

At his sublime best there are few better. Townsend can do things that other players wouldn't even see, let alone have the audacity to pull off. Quite simply, he's the most talented, most exciting Scottish player of his generation."

With Scotland going through some tough times in the 1990s, Townsend's finest season in the blue shirt came in 1999. He scored a try in every match as Scotland recorded wins over Wales (33-20), Ireland (30-13) and France (36-22). Although they fell to England at Twickenham by 24-21, Townsend still managed to get on the score sheet with a five-pointer. And when Wales ended England's Grand Slam dream in the tournament's final match, it meant Scotland had won the title, giving them the permanent accolade of 'reigning Five Nations champions' as the following year Italy joined the party and five became six.

Illustrious as Townsend's Scotland career has been, which includes two appearances as captain in 1996, against Italy and Australia, it was with the British & Irish Lions that he truly made his name on the world stage. As part of McGeechan's 1997 tourists to South Africa, Townsend starred in the first two Tests as the Lions forged an unassailable 2-0 lead. Mike Catt replaced Townsend in the third Test, but the job was already done. Townsend had been the ideal Lion, as Donald McRae wrote in his book Winter Colours: "He was the kind of Lion whom (Jim) Telfer and McGeechan had always wanted. A talented player who took risks, a player who relied more on instinct than caution. He made mistakes but he was not afraid to try different ideas. The coaches were emphatic that they needed more like Townsend, who were fresh and intelligent and open."

In the same book, Townsend also explained his approach to the game. "I love to run with the ball and look for the break," he said. "I love moving the ball out wide. If I didn't enjoy my rugby I'd retire. You've only got about ten years in the game so you have to enjoy it."

Townsend appeared in two World Cups for Scotland, losing at the quarter-final stage at both. New Zealand sent the Scots packing 30-18 in 1999 before Australia brought their 2003 campaign – and Townsend's international career as it turned out – to an end with a 33-16 win in Brisbane.

Scotland's Australian coach Matt Williams decided Townsend's Test career should come to an end at the age of 30 and this prompted the player to depart for pastures new in South Africa and France.

He returned to Scotland after those campaigns with the Sharks and Montpellier, and played a part in the Borders' Celtic League revival in the 2005-06 season. Now 33, Townsend started 2006 as Scotland's most capped player and has not totally ruled out a return to the Scotland squad, should his services ever be required.

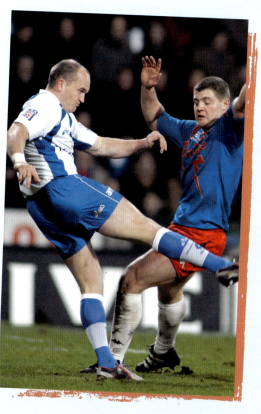

Legends of **RUGBY**

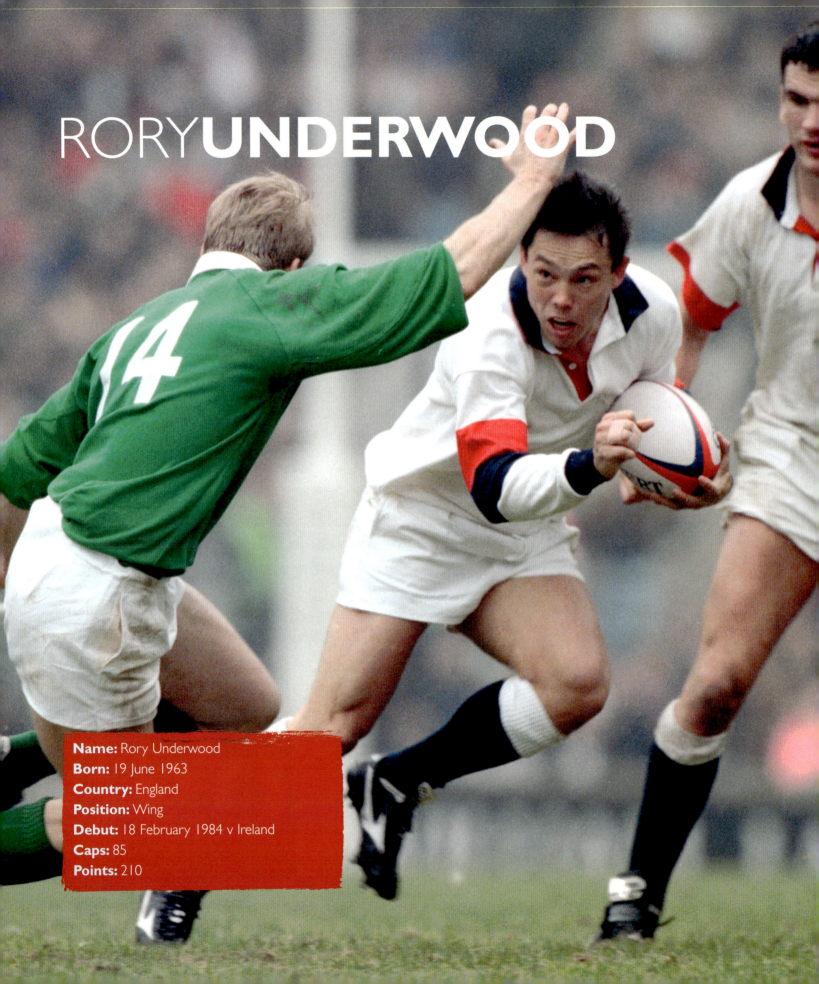

RORY**UNDERWOOD**

Name: Rory Underwood
Born: 19 June 1963
Country: England
Position: Wing
Debut: 18 February 1984 v Ireland
Caps: 85
Points: 210

RORY UNDERWOOD

To any fan of Leicester or England, the name Rory Underwood means one thing: tries. One of the deadliest finishers the English game has seen, the RAF pilot racked up a record 49 tries on the international stage and terrorised defences for fun during his club career with Leicester and then Bedford.

Educated at Barnard Castle School, Underwood played for Middlesbrough and Durham County before being snapped up by Leicester in 1983. It was there that he made his name. The year after signing for the East Midlands club, Underwood made his England debut in a 12-9 win over Ireland in the 1984 Five Nations. In his next International he set the try-counter running, although the excitement of the feat was quelled by the fact he was on the losing side, France winning 32-18 in Paris.

These were fraught times for England players and fans alike, as the side struggled to find any form in the championship. During Underwood's first four tournaments, the highest position they achieved was a miserable fourth. The form was reflected in the winger's try-poaching as he added just one more score to his tally during the period.

A runners-up spot in 1989 – when France were champions – did give some indication that better times lay ahead for England. Despite frequently suffering from a lack of ball, as England played a narrow game that suited their powerful forwards, Underwood's pace, strength and finishing ability was were getting him noticed. Further recognition duly came in the shape of a place on the 1989 British & Irish Lions tour to Australia. The Leicester flyer would play in all three Tests as the tourists won the series 2-1, despite having been brushed aside 30-12 by the Wallabies in the opener.

By this time, Underwood had already picked up a Courage League title (1988) and appeared in a Pilkington Cup final (1989) with Leicester, and increasingly he began to find his way to the try-line for his country too. Against Fiji in November 1989 he scored five tries and in the ensuing Five Nations campaign he grabbed four more, including a brace against Wales. Unfortunately for Underwood, England failed to fire in the Grand Slam decider against Scotland, and the title slipped from their grasp into the hands of the auld enemy.

England may have fallen at the last hurdle, but the following year they made amends. Four wins from four matches and another couple of tries from Underwood saw England record a first Grand Slam since 1980. It gave them the perfect warm-up to the World Cup that they would be hosting later that year.

That World Cup was to be a case of so near yet so far. Despite an opening-day defeat by New Zealand, wins over Italy (36-6) and the United States (37-9) in the pool stages, and knockout victories against France (19-10) and Scotland (9-6), took England into a Twickenham final against Australia. Underwood had been scoring freely throughout the tournament with three in the pool stages and a vital touchdown in the quarter-final with France.

In theory, with England opting for an expansive game in the final, the tactics should have led to more

BELOW
Rory Underwood celebrates England's Grand Slam win after defeating Scotland during the 1995 Five Nations, Twickenham.

RORY UNDERWOOD

tries for Underwood against the Wallabies. But the game plan famously careered down a blind alley and England went down 12-6 in arguably their most painful defeat in history.

Spirits were soon soaring again, however. England ran away with a second Grand Slam on the trot in the 1992 Five Nations. Scotland were swept away at Murrayfield 25-7, Ireland even more so at Twickenham (48-9), France offered little opposition even in Paris (31-13) and the Slam was completed in front of a home crowd against Wales, who succumbed 24-0. Yet again, Underwood's tries had been a key part, as he crossed the line in three of the four matches. And there was added satisfaction to the campaign, as brother Tony joined Rory in the team as the pair became the first brothers to play for England since 1938.

England were to be brought down to earth in 1993. Underwood had a quiet Five Nations, scoring just one try, as England's championship bid was derailed in only the second game as they lost 10-9 to Wales, Underwood being caught napping by Ieuan Evans for the critical score. A second defeat followed by Ireland in the final game to leave England trailing disappointingly in third spot.

On the plus side for Underwood, Leicester, with he and Tony on the wing, won the Pilkington Cup against Harlequins 23-16 at Twickenham, and he was picked for his second Lions tour, this time to New Zealand.

The trip would bring Underwood his first and only Test try for the Lions, as the tourists took the second Test 20-7 in Wellington. But it would ultimately end in a 2-1

Legends of **RUGBY**

FAR LEFT
Underwood runs with the ball for England during their 1995 Rugby World Cup match between New Zealand.

LEFT
Underwood steps around a tackle by Simon Geoghegan of Ireland during a Five Nations match between England and Ireland in Twickenham in 1996.

BELOW
Rory Underwood and brother Tony hold the Calcutta Cup and the Five Nations trophy, 1995.

series defeat as the All Blacks emphatically won the decider 30-13.

England returned to their championship-winning form two years later in 1995, storming to a third Grand Slam in five years. Underwood grabbed his first score at the Arms Park in a 23-9 win along the way and the clean sweep was completed against Scotland. Helping to atone for the disappointment of 1990, England gained revenge with a 24-12 win.

Underwood's swansong came in 1996 with his fourth Five Nations title and, while it didn't yield any more tries to add to his record-breaking tally of 49, it was a fitting end for one of the greatest England wingers of all -time. His 85 Tests (he also played in non-cap matches against Japan and the Soviet Union) make him one of the most capped players in history.

Having rattled up 134 tries in 236 first-team matches for Leicester, Underwood departed his beloved Welford Road in 1997 for Bedford Blues and helped them gain promotion to English rugby's top flight.

Legends of **RUGBY**

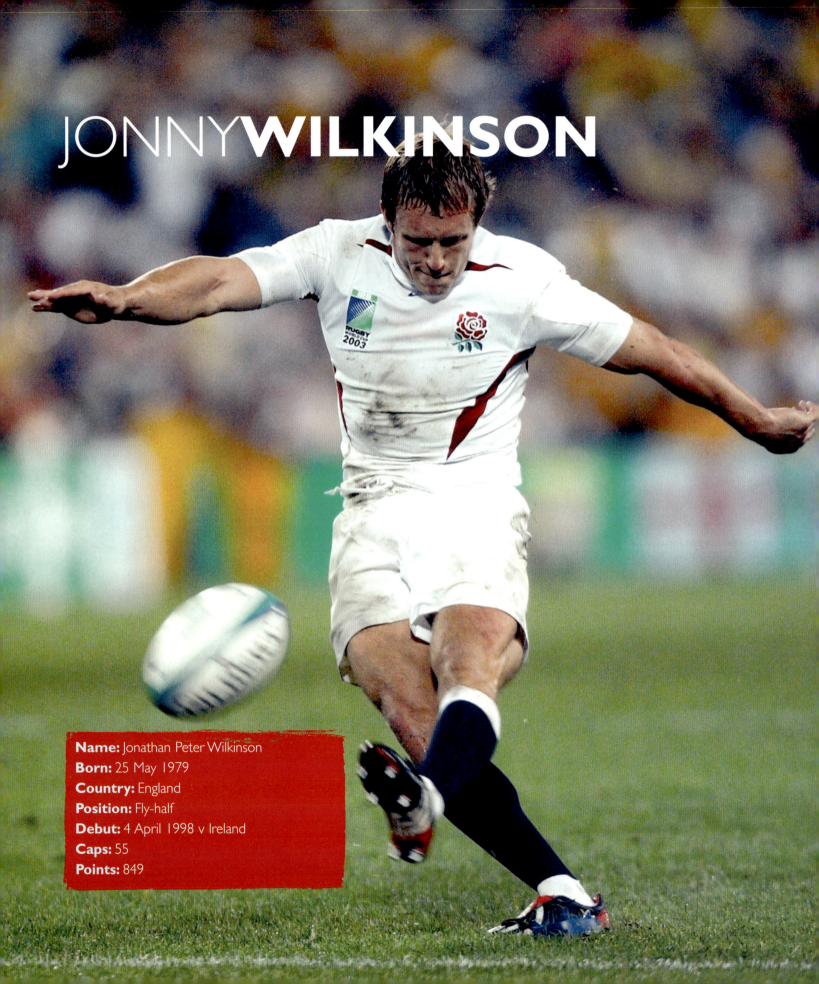

JONNY WILKINSON

Name: Jonathan Peter Wilkinson
Born: 25 May 1979
Country: England
Position: Fly-half
Debut: 4 April 1998 v Ireland
Caps: 55
Points: 849

JONNY WILKINSON

When Jonny Wilkinson kicked the winning drop-goal in the 2003 World Cup final, he had the sporting world at his feet. He was the world's most famous rugby player, the best outside-half and had just delivered the Webb Ellis Cup to Twickenham for the first time in history.

From then on things started to go wrong, with a list of injuries that would have finished most players. Shoulder, bicep, knee and groin injuries mounted one upon another, ensuring that, by the end of the 2006 Six Nations, he hadn't pulled on an England shirt since that famous day in Sydney nearly two-and-a-half years earlier.

Although Wilkinson was just 24 when that right-footed drop-goal bisected the uprights in Sydney's Olympic Stadium, he had already done enough to earn legendary status.

The boy from Surrey made his international debut at the age of 18, coming on as a substitute in the closing moments of England's 35-17 Five Nations win at home to Ireland in 1998 and becoming his country's youngest full international for 71 years.

And although his first start in the England No 10 shirt came in an infamous 76-0 defeat in Australia, the experience only intensified his determination to make it to the top.

After having a cameo role in the 1999 World Cup, he started to set the rugby world alight, beginning with a championship record of 78 points in the 2000 Six Nations, when he was just 20. That June he missed England's first-Test defeat by South Africa with food poisoning. Yet a week later he climbed off his sick bed to kick all 27 points as England won 27-22 in Bloemfontein, a performance described by coach Clive Woodward as "awesome".

By 2001, Wilkinson had become England's leading point-scorer of all time, surpassing his club coach Rob Andrew at Newcastle. The following year, he enhanced his reputation as one of the world's best players with a starring role in a trio of England wins over South Africa, New Zealand and Australia.

And once World Cup year cranked into gear he was unstoppable, inspiring England to a Grand Slam, with 77 points in the Six Nations, and summer wins over New Zealand and Australia, that set them up for victory in Sydney.

Even before the final against Australia, Wilkinson left an indelible mark, scoring all of England's 24 points in the semi-final win over France. He finished the final with 15 points and ended the tournament as top point-scorer with 113.

Wilkinson came under huge pressure during that World Cup in Australia. He became the biggest sports star in the country and saw his every move under scrutiny. The rest of the England team were in awe over the way his mental strength kept him on top and, once the Webb Ellis Cup was won, Martin Johnson had some special words of praise for Wilkinson.

"I can't say enough about Wilko," said England's skipper. "There is a lot of pressure on him and he gets built up to a degree where people expect superhuman stuff from him, and most of the stuff he does is verging on that.

BELOW
Wilkinson of England breaks through the South African defence during their match at Twickenham, 2000.

Legends of **RUGBY**

JONNY WILKINSON

To call him a kicker doesn't do him justice because the work he puts in on the field and in all aspects of his game is fantastic. He is a very special player, a very special person."

After Sydney, Wilkinson became one of the most recognisable faces in the sporting world and he even had the chance to play American Football. But when the offer came along the reaction of Woodward summed up Wilkinson's value to rugby.

"I wanted to create superstar players in rugby like Jonny and we've done that," Woodward said. "But we have to make sure we pay them. We could lose Jonny to American Football, for example, and we just can't do that. I wouldn't let that happen. People play sport because of people like Tiger Woods and David Beckham and Jonny Wilkinson."

An obsessive trainer in his early 20s, Wilkinson has admitted his routine played its part in his catalogue of injuries. Wilkinson said: "The reason this is happening is the shearing of the joints from the repetitive nature of the kicking. I understand that – I've put a lot of strain on myself. The two-hour kicking sessions will always be with me. If I have a problem with the kicking, I almost feel I have no choice, it's second nature to carry on until I've got it right.

But for years I've been compounding two-hour session upon two-hour session. I'm going to have to be a bit cuter now. I know I cannot afford to think like that every single day."

Andy Robinson's first act when becoming England coach in October 2004 was to appoint Wilkinson as England captain, taking over from Lawrence Dallaglio. But injury ensured he was never given the chance to wear the captain's armband for a second time, having led England against Italy in the 2003 Six Nations. "He is a natural leader," said Robinson, "and he consistently demonstrates the energy and commitment I feel is essential to be captain of England.

FAR LEFT
A Lion, in both Australia (2001) and New Zealand (2005), Wilkinson is already one of the world's greatest players.

LEFT
Wilkinson quickly became England's leading point scorer.

BELOW
Wilkinson in his Newcastle colours trying to evade Mike Catt, in the 2006 European Challenge Cup semi-final.

Jonny is in every way the right player to take on this challenge."

In 2002 he was awarded an MBE, becoming the youngest rugby union player to receive a New Year honour, in succession to Gareth Edwards, who was 27. An OBE followed for Wilkinson after the World Cup.

Despite his injury problems, he was fit enough to go on the 2005 Lions tour, where he won two caps to add to the three he won in a losing series in Australia in 2001. Selected in an unfamiliar role of centre against the All Blacks, he played the first Test but was taken off injured in the second. He was the only choice as 2003 BBC Sports Personality of the Year.

As England's 2006 summer tour approaches, Wilkinson has scored 817 points in 52 Tests for England, putting him sixth on the all-time list.

Legends of **RUGBY**

CHESTER WILLIAMS

The career of Chester Williams was never going to be an easy one. His country was taking its first tentative steps back into the world of Test rugby and it was doing so with a huge weight of expectation, by virtue of its status as one of the great rugby-playing nations in the world.

And it wasn't just the sporting world that had its eye on South Africa's Springboks. The Republic's long-time use of apartheid, a system of segregation on racial grounds, meant the world was looking on to discover if there really was change afoot in the Rainbow Nation.

Being the only black player in the traditionally all-white South African rugby team meant that Williams didn't just represent himself when he put on the green and gold jersey but the future of his country. It was an intense time to be involved in the Springbok set-up and Williams certainly wishes things had been different, as he explained in Donald McRae's book Winter Colours: "I want nothing more than to be seen as a rugby player. It's impossible. I'm always the 'Coloured Springbok' or the 'Black Pearl'. It's the same every year. I always wish I could just be another player. I want to go out there and try my best without having this pressure that I am playing on behalf of every single person in the 'New South Africa'.

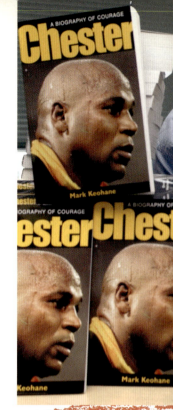

"But I understand. People want to see coloureds and blacks in the Springbok team. They want to use them to make a statement about the country. But, like every white guy in the side, I'm just an ordinary player who wants to do well for himself and his family and, in the end, for the country. That's it. It's hard to deal with the other stuff."

Despite his father playing rugby, as a child Williams showed little interest in following in his footsteps. "Rugby, in my young days, was something my dad played," he wrote in his autobiography Chester. "I wasn't interested in the game. My dad was a rugby player and that's where it ended. I had no heroes, I did not support Western Province or the Springboks. I did not keep scrapbooks or follow the big games closely."

That would change, of course, when, after playing a match in the same side as his son, Williams senior retired from rugby and effectively handed the baton to Chester. Once he began to play regularly, Chester caught the rugby bug and he ended up playing for Western Province. He made seven starts for his province in 1991 and 1992, and was selected for South Africa for the first time in 1993, making a try-scoring debut as the Springboks put Argentina to the sword 52-23 in Buenos Aires. Williams was the first black player to play for South Africa since Errol Tobias in the 1980s.

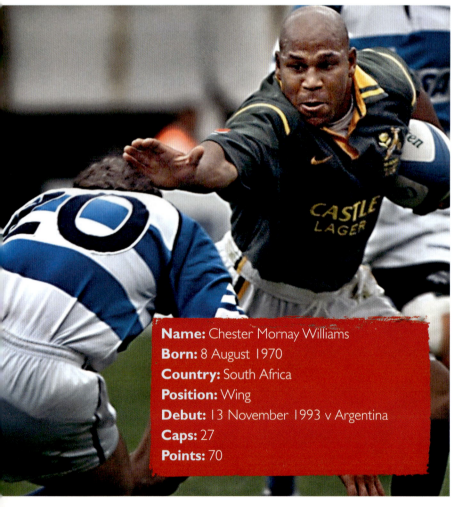

Name: Chester Mornay Williams
Born: 8 August 1970
Country: South Africa
Position: Wing
Debut: 13 November 1993 v Argentina
Caps: 27
Points: 70

CHESTER WILLIAMS

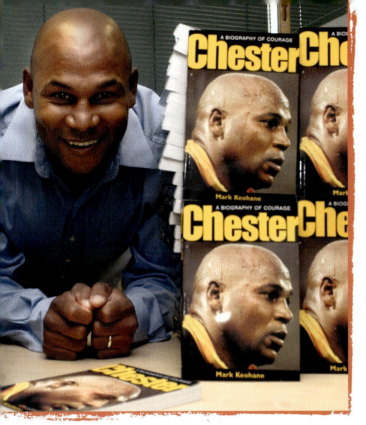

While seemingly popular within the squad, Williams maintained that he never truly felt part of the Afrikaans-dominated set-up. But that never seemed to affect his form on the pitch. His clinical finishing made him stand out as an international player in his own right, and the colour of his skin made no difference to that.

Scoring an average of a try a match in his early Test career, Williams was set to be part of South Africa's first-ever World Cup campaign in 1995, only for him to withdraw on the eve of the tournament with a hamstring injury.

Yet fate was to intervene as he was later recalled to the squad after fellow winger Pieter Hendriks was banned for 90 days for his part in a brawl that erupted in a pool match against Canada.

A World Cup has never been as important to a nation as that 1995 competition was to its hosts, South Africa. Desperate to prove to everyone how their country had changed, winning was the only option. Williams's call-up proved a real bonus for the host nation, as he acknowledged in his book, where he described himself as "the biggest marketing tool for the team during the World Cup".

He returned in grand style, scoring four tries as the Springboks thrashed Samoa 42-14 in the quarter-finals. A semi-final victory over France followed before Williams lined up in the historic team that accomplished the mission, with a 15-12 win in the final over the All Blacks.

Completing 1995 with a try in a 24-14 win over England later that year at Twickenham, Williams appeared to be on the crest of a wave.

But he would come crashing down. Injuries curtailed his international career and he started just four more Tests for South Africa, making a further seven appearances from the bench. On the last occasion that he made the 22-man match-day squad, against England in 2000, he didn't even make it onto the field as the Springboks lost 25-17 at Twickenham.

He retired from playing in 2001 and went on to coach South Africa's sevens side and the Cats.

Williams left a lasting impression, not only on South Africans but also rugby players the world over. Australian legend David Campese counts himself as a member of the Williams fan club, as he wrote in the foreword to Chester. "Unfortunately I played against Chester only once in the Super 10. Although I regret never having crossed paths with him at Test level, his reputation as a first-class winger was evident. He impressed me so much that he was the only South African whom I invited to play in my tribute game in Australia in 1994. The 1995 World Cup brought South Africa into the spotlight and Chester, along with the Springboks, played a style of rugby that the world will never forget. He embraced the opportunity and revealed a passion for rugby that encouraged respect from the rugby community, but more importantly, from the staunch South African rugby supporters."

LEFT
The former Springbok Chester Williams with copies of his biography in 2002.

BELOW
Williams on training ground, 1994.

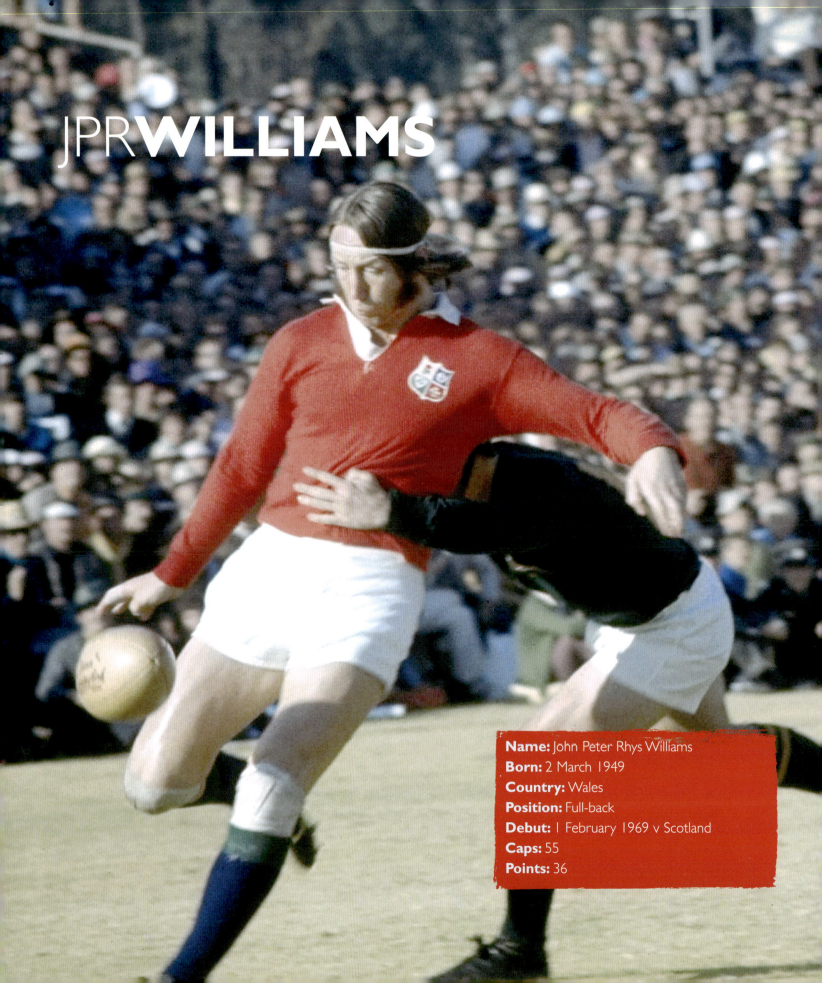

JPR WILLIAMS

Name: John Peter Rhys Williams
Born: 2 March 1949
Country: Wales
Position: Full-back
Debut: 1 February 1969 v Scotland
Caps: 55
Points: 36

JPR WILLIAMS

You know you've made it in the sporting world when people refer to you just by your first name or initials. Mention 'JPR' and everyone from Bridgend to Ballymena, from Cardiff to Christchurch, knows who you're taking about: John Peter Rhys Williams. JPR – so named to differentiate him from another John Williams in the Wales team, winger JJ – became a legend in the 1970s as a pivotal part of the Wales side that swept all before them in Europe. He was also one of the few men to play in all eight Lions Tests during the victorious tours of 1971 and 1974. An orthopaedic surgeon, JPR turned down the chance to make it three Lions tours in 1977 to focus on forthcoming medical exams.

Born in Cardiff, JPR played his club rugby for Bridgend and London Welsh, during a glittering career that brought 55 Wales caps, his list of honours including three Grand Slams and six Triple Crowns. In 45 Five Nations matches, he finished on the losing side just seven times, and not once against England.

Not a prolific try-scorer, JPR was so often the architect of tries for Wales and the Lions. His most memorable intervention came at Eden Park in 1971, when he landed a 50-yard drop-goal in the fourth Test that put the Lions into a 14-11 lead. The game ended 14-14 and the Lions had won the series 2-1.

And yet JPR could have been lost to another sport as he was an accomplished tennis player, making a huge impact at international level. JPR played tennis for Great Britain, and lifted the 1966 Junior Wimbledon. He also won a Welsh junior tennis title and played in the first professional tennis tournament, the British Open at Bournemouth, in 1968. However, all of Wales breathed a sigh of relief when JPR put down his racquet and picked up a rugby ball full time.

John Dawes, his team-mate in 1971, was unequivocal about JPR's influence both Wales and the Lions . "He was simply the best full-back of his type," said the former Lions captain. "He was a fearless tackler, had tremendous courage and was supremely confident. He couldn't spell the word loser. When he'd stay at my place and play cards with my kids, he'd never let them win, telling them, 'Let that be a lesson in life; you've got to win'."

Gareth Edwards is another to appreciate JPR's competitive instinct. In 1975, with Wales coasting towards a huge win over Ireland at Cardiff, Edwards threw out a loose pass that brought a consolation try for Willie Duggan. JPR gave Edwards a rollicking that went along the lines of: "How dare you let them cross my line!"

On another occasion, he retired from a match having had his face stamped on, only to stitch up the injury and return to the field!

JPR was first capped by Wales in 1969, as a 19-year-old, before embarking on his record-breaking career. He was to prove the scourge of England, beating them on no fewer than 14 occasions, three in junior rugby and 11 in Test matches, scoring five tries in the process. In fact, during his 12-year international career he only missed two games against England (in 1974 and 1980) and Wales lost them both.

BELOW
Williams stretching on the pitch, as he prepares for the 1971 Lions tour.

Legends of **RUGBY**

153

JPR WILLIAMS

His career had countless highlights but high on the list are his three Grand Slams, in 1971, 1976 and 1978, the latter secured after JPR made a crucial shoulder-barge tackle on Jean-Francois Gourdon near the corner flag. "Playing for Wales at Cardiff Arms Park in the Seventies was a hell of an experience," JPR said. "I suppose it must have been like being on a drug."

JPR was an initial inductee into the International Rugby Hall of Fame, in 1997.

"Perhaps it was just the way he played," explained former Wales captain Eddie Butler in The Observer. "He was so competitive and committed that he used to shut down all the instincts that have been triggers of fear ever since man found that unarmed combat with a sabre-toothed tiger was inadvisable.

"JPR was not big but he played huge. He had an unerring eye for the high ball and could sidestep as well as bounce juggernauts. He had a deft touch too and no moment was sweeter than when he dropped the goal from way back in the fourth Test against the All Blacks in 1971. The match was drawn; the Lions won the series 2-1, the only time they've ever beaten New Zealand."

Rock-solid in defence, it was through his skills as a counter-attacking full-back that JPR earned his worldwide reputation.

After Wales won the 1978 Grand Slam, JPR captained Wales five times, taking them through the 1979 Five Nations Triple Crown. He announced his retirement from international rugby, but later reversed his decision, playing against New Zealand in the autumn of 1980 and then England and Scotland in the 1981 Five Nations. He was dropped after the defeat at Murrayfield, a sad way to bow out, but his rugby-playing days were to last much, much longer.

His tremendous fitness levels meant that even at 48 he was still turning out for Tondu 3rds, unable to

Legends of **RUGBY**

FAR LEFT
Williams congratulates Bill Beaumont after Wales took on England.

LEFT JPR Williams playing for The Lions is challenged by a player from Transvaal during their tour of South Africa in 1974.

BELOW JPR was honoured by the Queen in 1977, being made an MBE. Alongside him are footballer Tommy Smith and tennis player Roger Taylor.

give up the game he loves. "Some people say I'm mad but I'm loving every minute of it. I'll have to retire when I'm 50, but I will continue to play competitive squash," said JPR at the time.

"They wouldn't pick me at openside flanker until the cup match – they said I'm too slow – so normally I pack down at No 8 or blindside.

"At junior level the rugby is like the game I used to play. The refreshing thing is that the players aren't too full of themselves, unlike some at senior level."

A product of Millfield School, along with Edwards, JPR graduated to veterans' rugby, making several appearances at the Bermuda Classic. We weren't going to get rid of him that easily and thank goodness for that!

Legends of **RUGBY**

KEITH WOOD

Injuries played far too big a role in the career of the 'flying potato' that was Keith Wood, and he should have won more than the 58 caps he managed from 1994 to 2003. The son of an Ireland international (Gordon Wood won 29 caps at prop), Wood's playing days began with Garryowen, where he won titles in 1992 and 1994 before accepting an offer to join English club Harlequins.

Enjoying some success at club level with the London side, Wood had a tough start to life with Ireland. He sat on the bench during the 1994 Five Nations and had to watch as, first up, his team-mates were hammered 35-15 by France. His Ireland debut followed on the summer tour to Australia, where his passion and all-action style in a losing cause won him the admiration of the Aussie public.

The next season he made his Five Nations debut in the 20-8 defeat by England at Lansdowne Road. Wood's early record for Ireland in the Five Nations read: played 11, won one, lost 10. He experienced life at the bottom as Ireland collected the wooden spoon three seasons in succession from 1996. The following year they dragged themselves up to fourth. In the book Five Go To War, Wood admitted that despite the lack of initial success, he never fell out of love with the competition: "In terms of success, the tournament has been less than favourable to me. My first win came against Wales at Wembley in 1999. I played my first Five Nations match in 1995. Yet after all those years of disappointment I love it all the more. It must be the masochist in me. Months after breaking my duck, I can still feel the glow of success emanating from that one win. Just one win! God only knows how I would react if we were to win the Championship."

Luckily for Wood, while he waited for success in the Five Nations, he had the small matter of the 1997 Lions tour to South Africa to take his mind off things. Starting in the crucial first two Tests (he missed only the third match, a dead rubber as the Lions had tied up the series), Wood was an influential figure not just for his work rate on the pitch but for the way he encouraged the camaraderie off it. Donald McRae was one of many to be impressed by Wood, as he wrote in Winter Colours. "Keith Wood personified what was best about the Lions. He was outrageously passionate and committed. But he also listened as well as he talked. And whether the Lions were in Vanderbylpark or in Durban, I had my most

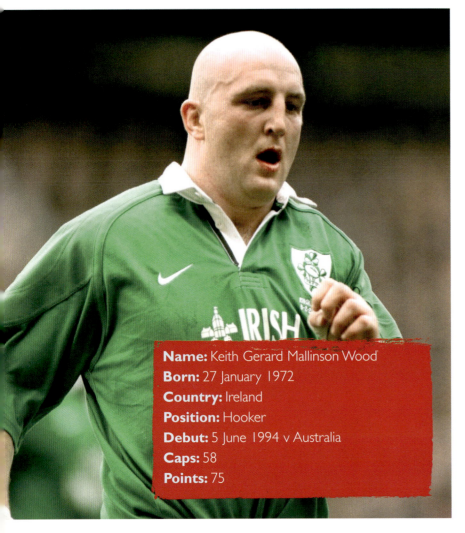

Name: Keith Gerard Mallinson Wood
Born: 27 January 1972
Country: Ireland
Position: Hooker
Debut: 5 June 1994 v Australia
Caps: 58
Points: 75

Legends of **RUGBY**

KEITH WOOD

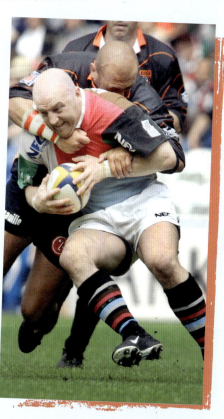

LEFT
Wood scored an incredible number of tries for a hooker, grabbing 75 points in his 58 Tests.

BELOW
Wood moved to Harlequins, here helping them win the European Shield in 2001.

to a Heineken Cup victory. He almost succeeded, too, as Munster were beaten 9-8 in the final by Northampton. He returned to Harlequins the next season.

Life got even better for Ireland in the 2001 Six Nations. Although Wood was missing for three of the matches, he featured in the 41-22 win over Italy and the 22-15 defeat of France. In a tournament disrupted by a foot-and-mouth crisis, England went to Dublin in the autumn in search of their first Grand Slam of the professional era. Despite being hot favourites, they never recovered from a 17th-minute try by Wood, who thundered over from a lineout move, and Ireland were left to celebrate a 20-14 success. The Irish lost out for the title to England on points difference. It was the closest Wood ever got to the Six Nations crown.

A Lions tour was also on the agenda for 2001 and again Wood was an automatic selection for the trip to Australia. He played in all three Tests but, unlike in South Africa, this time the series was lost 2-1.

As a final stop on Wood's roller-coaster Test exploits, he led Ireland to the World Cup in Australia. Facing Fabian Galthie's France in the quarter-final, the losing captain faced a disappointing end to their international career. Sadly for Wood, Galthie would carry on to play another match as Ireland crashed 43-21 and the Test arena bade farewell to one of its biggest characters.

"My desire's still there. I'd like to play for another 10 years if I had the chance," said Wood at the time. "The heart is willing, the head is willing, but the body's had enough."

stimulating conversations with him. He was as ready to entertain me with stories about rugby fervour in Limerick as he was keen to hear about the wild streets of Johannesburg. He would tell me about some of his witty encounters with South African girls and then a thing or two about the ancient art of falconry. That was Keith Wood, a bald but brilliant 25-year-old – an all-round sort of guy. But, above all else, he was a son of Limerick."

Eager as Wood was to help the Lions bond as a unit, however, he was quick to point out that it would be a different story when they all returned home. "I've told these new pals of mine that when we next play against each other, I'm going to kick them in the nuts if I get the chance!" he said. "I expect them to do the same to me and have a pint with me afterwards."

As a player, Wood led from the front, charging around the field and scoring an obscene number of tries for a front-row forward – he managed 15 for Ireland, including four in a 1999 World Cup match against the USA.

In 2000, despite an opening-day hammering by England (50-18), Wood led his side to third spot in the first Six Nations thanks to three victories, the most notable of which was an epic 27-25 win over the French – Ireland's first win in Paris for 28 years.

That same year, Wood had returned to Ireland to play one season with Munster in an attempt to inspire them

Legends of **RUGBY**

Legends of **RUGBY**

Legends of **RUGBY**

THE PICTURES IN THIS BOOK WERE PROVIDED COURTESY OF THE FOLLOWING:

GETTY**IMAGES**
101 Bayham Street, London NW1 0AG

EMPICS
www.empics.com

Concept and Art Direction:
VANESSA and KEVIN**GARDNER**

Creative and Artwork: KEVIN**GARDNER**

Image research: ELLIE**CHARLESTON**

PUBLISHED BY GREEN UMBRELLA PUBLISHING

Publishers:
JULES**GAMMOND** and VANESSA**GARDNER**

Written by: PAUL**MORGAN** and ALEX**MEAD**